WOODEN SHIPS ON
WINYAH BAY

WOODEN SHIPS ON
WINYAH BAY

Robert McAlister

Charleston · London

THE
History
PRESS

Published by The History Press
Charleston, SC 29403
www.historypress.net

Front cover, top: Courtesy of the Georgetown County Museum.
Back cover: Courtesy of the Georgetown County Digital Library.

First published 2011

Manufactured in the United States

ISBN 978.1.60949.353.0

Library of Congress Cataloging-in-Publication Data
McAlister, Robert.
Wooden ships on Winyah Bay / Robert McAlister.
p. cm.
Includes bibliographical references and index.
ISBN 978-1-60949-353-0
1. Ships, Wooden--South Carolina--Winyah Bay. 2. Sailing ships--South Carolina--Winyah
Bay. 3. Sailboats--South Carolina--Winyah Bay. 4. Georgetown (S.C.)--History, Naval. 5.
Winyah Bay (S.C.)--History. I. Title.
VM144.M377 2011
623.8'440975789--dc23
2011018255

CONTENTS

FOREWORD

Members of the Gullah community often say "the water brought us." While most of us may not be able to say the same, we can certainly say the water has sustained us. Water, and more specifically, the ocean and rivers, was the lifeblood of existence for centuries for virtually everyone and provided a route for exploration of the world. From earliest times, man used wood to make vessels to travel that route from one continent to another, to traverse the environment in which he settled and to provide transportation for trading of resources, goods and food. The boats that man has made from wood have always been of interest to mariners, scholars and everyday sailors. To add to the lore, Mac McAlister's book *Wooden Ships on Winyah Bay* is a great resource for individuals curious about the churnings of the sea and the early maritime history of Winyah Bay and the Georgetown, South Carolina area.

I first met Mac through my connection to the Harbor Historical Association, which sponsors the annual Wooden Boat Show in Georgetown. The show is held on the third Saturday in October and is considered the preeminent wooden boat show in the Southeast. Mac has been a staunch supporter of the show for years, and my first conversation with him explained why. Mac and his wife, Mary, lived on a barge in Europe and have sailed to exotic locations in their own wooden vessel. Our talk made me realize that he has lived the way so many of us want to. He has a love of and respect for the sea, and the research he has uncovered for this book exemplifies that he knows not only the water but also, and of more importance, the wooden boats about which he writes. Mac has visited many maritime museums and has offered helpful suggestions for our own Georgetown County Maritime Museum.

I grew up fishing the waters around Winyah Bay and learned to sail while I was at the College of Charleston. Upon graduation, I bought my own sailboat, though not wooden, to sail the bay with dreams of eventually sailing to the Bahamas. I took my parents out for the maiden voyage of my new boat. My unseaworthy father thought he would be helpful and untied every dock line of the unmanned vessel, and I watched in horror as the boat drifted away. How I wish I had known Mac at the time, as I would have made sure he was present to make the maiden voyage go smoothly. My work as a senior interpreter at Hobcaw Barony for the past fourteen years has enabled me to intimately watch Winyah Bay and to observe its frequent changes from the safety of the shore. So much of the history of Hobcaw Barony is influenced by the tumultuous waters of the bay and the ships and men and women who sailed near its shore.

My fascination with wooden boats began as a young child. My father was restoring our house and always had extra blocks of wood. I coveted each block and, on many occasions, nailed together twenty or more pieces into what my young mind thought was the most magnificent wooden ship. In no way, shape or form did these constructions resemble anything close to a ship, and had any of them seen the water, all would have immediately sunk, to my dismay. As I grew older, trips to Maine helped me discover what true wooden ships were. Each trip resulted in my bringing home several model ship kits. My dream of actually sailing the seas had begun in earnest.

In the pages of his wonderful book, *Wooden Ships on Winyah Bay*, Mac McAlister uncovers stories of the real men and ships that lived my dream. The book covers the years 1500 to the present. He begins with the simplest craft known at the time, a wooden dugout canoe used by Native Americans to access creeks and rivers for oysters, clams and fish. The European explorers brought larger ships to our continent, and Mac describes several with multiple masts that plied Winyah Bay at some point during a voyage. The waters of the bay provided a livelihood for many people when large ships were in decline. For some individuals, the water provided income from shrimping, while the livelihood of others came from fishing for the prized caviar from the Atlantic sturgeon. Even as the commercial fishing industry waned, workers still enjoyed their own pleasure boats. Fascinating photographs accompany the text to provide the reader with a true image of these handcrafted vessels and how they were used and celebrated. Mac's research uncovers personal information about the captains and their crews, as well as the unfortunate ending in a watery grave of so many of their craft. Because of the maintenance required for those that survived, few large wooden ships are extant, and what can mostly be found today are the smaller wooden pleasure boats.

Reading *Wooden Ships on Winyah Bay* unveils the hardships of life at sea as well as the camaraderie that all lovers of boats enjoy. Here you will learn about the beginning and decline of shipping in the Georgetown, South Carolina region, as well as the concomitant history of a plantation bordering Winyah Bay. Let the water take you somewhere and sustain you. As you read Mac McAlister's enlightening history of wooden ships, you'll be taking your own navigational adventure. You may decide that a child's little wooden blocks and a dream make the safest sailing trips.

Richard Manning Camlin III
Georgetown County Maritime Museum

PREFACE AND
ACKNOWLEDGEMENTS

I first became interested in the maritime history of Georgetown in 1974, when I visited the Georgetown County Library and discovered a pile of old photographs on an open shelf. I picked through them and borrowed twenty-five of the nautical photographs to copy and display in the lobby of the Belle Isle Yacht Club in Georgetown. These photographs were part of a collection of photographs that Mayor William Doyle Morgan authorized to be taken between 1890 and 1915, showing various scenes of Georgetown life. Subsequently, I became more interested as I learned about the ships and characters that contributed to the unique history of Winyah Bay. Many books and articles have been written about specific wooden boats, ships and characters of this area. I wanted to describe the overall maritime history of the Winyah Bay region and complete the story before all memory of its wooden ships disappears.

I have received great help and encouragement with this project from many people. Julie Warren, project manager for the Georgetown County Digital Library, and others of the Georgetown County Library staff have been very patient and helpful in scanning and copying many images. Richard Camlin and Sally Swineford of the Georgetown Wooden Boat Show have been most helpful. I am grateful to Ginny and Michael Prevost for the use of early photographs by the Kaminski family. I am grateful to Glennie Tarbox for use of the Tarbox Collection of photographs and for stories about the fishing industry. Joe Cathou, Ronnie Campbell and Jerry Caines allowed me to use photos that were taken during the time Rene Cathou was alive. Jill Santopietro, curator of the Georgetown County Museum, Bud Hill of the McClellanville Museum and Jim Fitch at the Prevost Gallery helped me look through their collections. Conversations with Ronnie Campbell, Laura and Ernest Meyer, Albert Jones and Jerry and Roy Caines have led to many stories about Georgetown's nautical history. Ruth and David Ross have provided much encouragement and have helped immensely with editing the text. My wife, Mary Prevost Shower McAlister, took several of the photographs and made many helpful suggestions, besides being first mate for all of the voyages we have made. I am grateful to Phil and Jill Gordon of Falmouth, England, and all of our other friends in Cornwall, who increased my appreciation of wooden boats. I thank my contact editor, Jessica Berzon, and the rest of the staff at The History Press for their help.

CHAPTER I

WINYAH BAY FROM 1500 TO 1865

The Winyah, or Winyaw, were an Indian tribe who had, for more than one thousand years, fished and hunted along the shores of a protected bay, behind the shifting sands of a shallow, narrow inlet to the Atlantic Ocean. This bay was fifteen miles long and as much as a mile wide in places, bordered by beaches, salt marshes and flat lowlands that were covered by virgin forests of tall longleaf pines, cypress and cedar trees. The bay was located near latitude 33 degrees, 16 minutes north, longitude 79 degrees, 11 minutes west, or about fifty miles north of what would become Charleston, South Carolina. When the Spanish explorer Lucas Vasquez de Allyon sailed into the same bay in 1526, his ships were met by Winyah Indians paddling long cypress dugout canoes. Six months later, one of Allyon's galleons, the *Capitana*, went aground in the inlet and was abandoned when the Spanish gave up their attempts to find gold and returned to Hispaniola.

English traders sailed into the same inlet before 1700 and began to trade with the Winyah Indians and other tribes in the area. England had claimed all of the territory for themselves, and in 1663, King Charles II bestowed on eight of his friends who had done him favors the title of Lords Proprietors, with authority to govern the Carolina provinces. In 1711, the Lords Proprietors gave large grants of land along the shores of the Winyah Bay, including the same land where the Winyah Indians had lived for centuries, to a few wealthy English settlers. The English took the land away from the Winyahs, and by 1720, all Indians near the bay had been killed, enslaved or

Above: An 1802 Drayton chart of Winyah Bay showing shoals at the mouth and a canal cut through North Island. The canal was opposed by North Island summer residents and was not completed. One hundred years later, the present entrance to Winyah Bay was deepened, and stone jetties were constructed to protect it. *Taken from* A View of South Carolina *by Governor John Drayton.*

Right: Portion of an 1802 Drayton map of South Carolina from Georgetown to Charleston. *Taken from* A View of South Carolina *by Governor John Drayton.*

driven away. Scatterings of decorated pottery shards and the name Winyah Bay are all that remain to show that they were ever there.

In 1733, English settlers established a town at the western end of Winyah Bay, fifteen miles from the ocean, and named it Georgetown. Another wealthy landowner tried, in 1737, to establish a second town closer to the mouth of Winyah Bay, in a location "whereon 500 Sail of Vessel may ride before the said Town," but Smith's Town never materialized. Georgetown was laid out along the north shore of the Sampit River, which extended westward from Winyah Bay. Other rivers—the Waccamaw, the Pee Dee and the Black—flowed into Winyah Bay near Georgetown. These rivers were navigable for many miles into the interior of the Carolinas, and English and French Huguenot settlers built houses and farms along their banks.

Square-rigged ships arrived from England and anchored in Winyah Bay, bringing representatives of the colonial government. These aristocrats and wealthy men of trade recognized one thing that this land offered and that England needed: an abundance of tall, straight trees stout enough and tall enough for masts of the largest ships of the English fleet. From that time on, the swamps and forests nearest the bay and the rivers feeding it began to be stripped of longleaf pines over one hundred feet tall and four feet in diameter; eight-foot-thick cypress trees one thousand years old; and three-hundred-year-old live oaks with gnarled limbs, perfectly shaped for the ribs and knees of English ships. The trees that were cut down would never be replaced and would disappear from the coastal lands of South Carolina and other southern states during the next two hundred years, making fortunes for those who cut and shipped them away but leaving behind a land of low, sandy pine barrens and eroding riverbanks that carried much silt into Winyah Bay.

Settlers cut the trees they needed to build small boats to take their produce into Georgetown and to bring supplies back to their farms. Archaeologists discovered the remains of a vessel from the 1740s on the bottom of the Black River, the earliest sailing craft found so far in America. It was fifty feet long, with provision for a two-masted rig. The hull was narrow, flat bottom amidships, tapering out at each end. The shallow hull was built of live oak framing members and wide pine planks. Known as the Brown's Ferry Vessel, it was loaded with a cargo of twenty-five tons of bricks. Among the artifacts aboard the vessel was a navigation quadrant, which indicated that the vessel was probably sailed off shore between Georgetown and Charles Town. The restored remains of the vessel are displayed in the old Kaminski Hardware Building in Georgetown.

Remains of the 1740 Brown's Ferry Vessel and a model of the vessel. *Photo by the author.*

By 1730, the settlers who owned tracts of land along the riverbanks had discovered a demand for rice in England and had learned that the tidal freshwater swamps along the rivers were suitable for growing rice. They learned from West African slaves how to irrigate the rice fields at appropriate times by using the tides to flood the fields with fresh water from the rivers. To accomplish the gigantic and backbreaking tasks of clearing and diking thousands of acres of rice fields, the planters bought thousands of black slaves from the West Indies and Africa and brought them to South Carolina aboard cramped slave ships, such as *Le Concorde*. *Le Concorde* was an early eighteenth-century cargo ship converted to transport slaves. The ship was later captured by the notorious pirate Edward Teach, or Blackbeard, who changed the ship's name to *Queen Anne's Revenge* and menaced the Carolina coast with her until the ship was wrecked at New Topsail Inlet, North Carolina, in 1718.

Many of the slaves who were brought to the rice plantations around Georgetown were captured in the interior of Africa and confined in British slave castles, such as the one on Bunce Island in Sierra Leone. A typical advertisement in a Charles Town newspaper of 1769 stated, "On Thursday the 3rd day of August a cargo of ninety-four prime, healthy Negroes, consisting of thirty-nine men, fifteen boys, and sixteen girls. Just arrived in the Brigantine *Dembia*, Francis Bare Master, from Sierra Leone." Slaves were treated as beasts of burden by their owners and were set to work in the swamps along the rivers by slave drivers. They cleared the swamps of trees and stumps, hand dug hundreds of miles of dikes and canals to contain the rice fields and planted, tended and harvested the rice. Rice was packed in six-hundred-pound barrels called tierces, loaded on flat-bottomed barges and poled, rowed and sailed down the rivers by slaves to Georgetown. Many of the smaller wooden barges and flats were built by plantation slaves.

Georgetown had a thriving shipbuilding industry from 1740 to about 1760. More than thirty vessels listed Georgetown as their site of construction during this period. The largest ship listed was the 180-ton *Francis*, built in 1751, probably by Benjamin Darling, since his was the largest shipyard in Georgetown during this period.

Most of the rice was loaded aboard small sloops or schooners, which sailed out of Winyah Bay to Charles Town, where there were rice mills. The processed rice was loaded aboard larger English ships and exported to northern cities or to Europe. More than half of the rice produced in colonial America was grown near Georgetown. During the 1740s, another valuable crop, indigo, which was used to dye cloth, was grown on some plantations. Preference was given to the Georgetown colonists to grow and export indigo to England.

The rice and indigo planters became the richest men in South Carolina and were among the richest in colonial America. Trying to copy the aristocracy of England, the planters near Georgetown built palatial town homes in the more cosmopolitan city of Charles Town. They also built homes on the beaches at Pawleys Island and North Island to escape the summer heat and malaria at their plantations, leaving overseers to manage the work of the slaves. By the time of the American Revolution, there were many more slaves than white people on the plantations surrounding Georgetown.

When America declared independence from England in 1776, France became an ally of America. A member of one of France's wealthiest and most influential families, the nineteen-year-old Marquis de Lafayette decided to join Washington's army and fight the British. He purchased a 268-ton merchant ship in France, *La Victoire*, and accompanied by General Baron De Kalb and others, he set sail for Charles Town. Lafayette didn't tell his seventeen-year-old wife, who was expecting their second child, that he was leaving because her powerful nobleman father would have tried to stop him from going. On June 13, 1777, fearing that Charles Town might be blockaded by British ships, *La Victoire* sailed farther north and entered Winyah Bay. She anchored near North Island, a narrow sandy barrier island separating Winyah Bay from the ocean and a beach resort for some of the planters. Lafayette was rowed ashore in the ship's jolly boat. According to Harlow Unger's book *Lafayette*:

> *It was ten o'clock at night before they reached the northern tip of the island and found some unintelligible black slaves combing for oysters. When the outgoing tide left the jolly boat mired in mud, Lafayette and the others climbed into the oyster boat—a crude, hand hewn flat-bottomed craft. The slaves rowed them along the shore until a beam of light from their master's house flickered through the tall marsh grasses. It was midnight when they stumbled ashore.*

Lafayette was greeted by planter Benjamin Huger, at whose summer home on North Island he spent his first night in America. Taking no chances that their ship might be captured by the British, Lafayette and De Kalb were ferried across Winyah Bay the following day and slogged their way through alligator-infested swamps on horseback and on foot to Charles Town, arriving three days later "in wretched condition." Meanwhile, *La Victoire* avoided the blockade and anchored in Charles Town Harbor the day after Lafayette arrived. Later in June, *La Victoire* got underway for her return voyage to France but bilged on the Charles Town bar and was lost. After two weeks of entertainment in Charlestown, Lafayette and his company made an overland journey to Philadelphia, where he joined Washington's army. He was made general and fought bravely in the American Revolution. General De Kalb was killed at the Battle of Camden, South Carolina.

The first ship commanded by John Paul Jones, father of the U.S. Navy, was the sloop *Providence*. Jones was captain of the *Providence* from 1776 until late 1777, when he turned command of the ship over to Captain Rathbun. On Thanksgiving Day 1777, Captain Rathbun and the *Providence* fought and captured the British privateer *Governor Tryon* off the South Carolina coast. He brought the captured vessel into Georgetown as a prize. Privateers were independently owned warships operated for the purpose of capturing vessels of enemy countries and collecting money from the sale of the captured vessels and their cargo. Privateers had to have the approval, "Letters of Marque," of their home country's government.

South Carolina, like several other states, had its own independent navy during the Revolution, commanded by Commodore Alexander Gillon of Charles Town. Since South Carolina had almost no ships, Gillon was sent to Europe by the state in 1779 to buy two or three warships. After much searching, he found a newly constructed frigate in Amsterdam, *L'Indien*, which he was able to lease from her owner, the Chevalier de Luxembourg. The frigate was 168 feet long and carried forty cannons. She was to be the largest warship under American command during the Revolution. Gillon renamed her *South Carolina* and made ready to send his five-hundred-man crew of sailors and marines into battle. However, he discovered that the depth of water along the route where *South Carolina* had to travel averaged only 13 feet, but his loaded ship drew 22 feet. He had no choice but to unload *South Carolina*, strip off all masts and rigging, pull her over on her side and have her towed for seventy miles to the sea, much to the amusement of Dutch onlookers. By that time it was winter, an unfit time for getting underway.

Gillon and *South Carolina* finally got underway in the spring of 1781, at which time he had run out of his and the state's money and credit. Gillon and *South Carolina* had a few other unfortunate experiences that kept him from ever tying up in a South Carolina port. In December 1781, Gillon was in sight of Cape Romain, headed for Charles Town. He discovered that Charles Town was in the hands of the British, so Gillon sailed *South Carolina* to Havana and aided the Spanish in a campaign to take Nassau from the British. Finally, in 1782, he sailed for Philadelphia and along the way captured a small Bahamian schooner, which he sent into Georgetown as a prize. Arriving in Philadelphia aboard the impressive *South Carolina*, Gillon was met by lawyers representing the Chevalier de Luxembourg, who claimed he had violated the lease and would be jailed. Gillon turned *South Carolina* over to an associate, Captain Joyner, and instructed him to put to sea and capture as many prizes as possible. Gillon escaped by land to Charles Town, where he was hailed as a naval hero for *South Carolina*'s part in the capture of Nassau. Somehow, he was able to avoid personal liability for the millions of dollars of debt still owed to the *South Carolina*'s creditors all over Europe. Meanwhile, Captain Joyner put to sea in *South Carolina* and was promptly attacked by three British frigates, *Diomede*, *Astrea* and *Quebec*, and forced to surrender. *South Carolina* was towed into New York as a British prize just before the war ended. After the war, she was sailed back to England and not heard of again, except for multitudes of claims against Gillon and the State of South Carolina that continued to pour in for the next fifty years.

After the Revolution, the rice planters of South Carolina's Lowcountry continued to prosper, even though the English market for indigo was lost. Shipments of rough, unprocessed rice were carried from Georgetown to Charleston in small coastal schooners and brigs, which were subject to storms in the Atlantic, particularly off Cape Romain. A safer route would be through inland creeks behind the ocean, if a canal could be built to connect the Santee River to the Cooper River, which flowed into Charleston. In 1790, a group of Charleston planters, politicians and Revolutionary War generals decided, as a business venture, to build the Santee Canal, joining the Santee to the Cooper. Construction of the canal started in 1793 and took an average yearly crew of seven hundred slaves seven years to build, at a cost three times more than the original estimate. The twenty-two-mile canal had twelve large masonry locks to raise boats and barges from the Santee River to a flat summit at the canal's highest elevation and then to lower them into the Cooper River.

Christian Senf, a Swedish engineer who had fought for the British and been captured, was made chief engineer of South Carolina at the end of the war. He supervised the design and construction of the canal. Senf, a very opinionated engineer, selected a route for the canal that would prove to be the most expensive one, and also the most difficult route to hold water in times of drought. When the canal was finally completed in 1800, it was the first and longest summit canal in the United States. Shallow draft boats and barges as long as fifty feet, loaded with rice, cotton or naval stores, could travel from Winyah Bay, through Mosquito Creek to the Santee River, up the river and through the Santee Canal to the Cooper River and down that river to Charleston. Most of the traffic in the canal, however, consisted of cotton bales on flat wooden barges, poled down the Santee River from plantations far upstream, to and through the Santee Canal and down to Charleston for export. The Santee Canal was in operation for a little over forty years but suffered problems of silting, leaking, lack of water and financial failure. It was abandoned in 1850, when railroads had been built that could handle freight more cheaply. An overgrown ditch and the massive brick ruins of a lock are all that remain of the canal. There is an excellent museum in Moncks Corner, South Carolina, devoted to the Santee Canal.

After the French Revolution of 1789, relations between France and the United States soured for a time, and French privateers began to prey on American merchant ships. On August 1, 1799, the schooner *Nancy* left Georgetown with a cargo of cattle, hogs, poultry, tobacco, provisions and lumber, bound for Cape Francois, Haiti. Captain Lawson owned the cargo and a share of the schooner. On August 26, the schooner was seized by the French privateer *La Bayonaissie* and taken to Puerto Rico. Captain Lawson was forced to abandon his ship and property and to return to Georgetown. The *Nancy* and her cargo were taken to Guadeloupe and sold.

Ships entering Winyah Bay were and still are—except for the four-year period of the Civil War when the light was extinguished—guided in by the

The 1811 Georgetown Lighthouse, lighthouse keeper's house and dance hall, where Georgetonians gathered for amusement on North Island in the early 1900s. *Courtesy of Georgetown County Digital Library, Tarbox Collection.*

flashes of Georgetown Light, an eighty-foot-tall circular masonry tower. The present lighthouse was constructed in 1811 on the east end of North Island. It replaced an earlier wooden tower. The entrance to Winyah Bay was always shallow and shifting, and vessels with a draft of over eight feet had to wait for high tide to cross the bar. Twice-daily high tides raise the water level in the bay about five feet. During the War of 1812, a garrison of soldiers was stationed on North Island to guard the entrance but was not called on to fight. The hundred or so planters and their families who lived in North Island summer homes would sometimes gather near the lighthouse to picnic and watch the maneuvers and parades of the soldiers.

One of the summer residents of North Island was Peter Horry, a rice planter whose plantation was along the shore of Winyah Bay. Horry was a Revolutionary War general who served under General Francis Marion, the famous Swamp Fox. After the war, Horry wrote a biography of Marion. According to Horry, Francis Marion was born at Winyah in 1732. At the age of sixteen, Marion left his home and went to sea as a sailor on a small Georgetown vessel. On Marion's first voyage, the ship was struck and sunk by a whale. The crew of six escaped in the jolly boat but with no provisions other than the ship's dog. The dog was eaten, but two of the crew died of starvation. A passing vessel finally rescued the survivors, including Marion, and returned them to Georgetown. That was the end of Francis Marion's seagoing career.

Another planter who had a summer home on North Island was South Carolina Governor William Alston. In 1801, he married Theodosia, the eighteen-year-old daughter of Aaron Burr. Theodosia moved from New York to William Alston's hot, humid plantation on the Waccamaw River, where she was not happy. In 1812, eight years after Aaron Burr's duel with Alexander Hamilton, Theodosia decided to visit her devoted father in New York. Theodosia was escorted to Georgetown to meet her ship at the Red Store Wharf, a 1765 warehouse and tavern at the end of Cannon Street where ships tied up. Theodosia boarded the sixty-eight-foot schooner *Patriot* as a passenger and set sail for New York. The *Patriot* foundered off Cape Hatteras in a gale, but the exact details of Theodosia's death remain a mystery. In 1822, the surge from a hurricane covered North Island and washed away almost all of the summer homes. Over one hundred people, mostly slaves, were drowned. Most of the houses were quickly rebuilt.

The rice plantations along the Pee Dee, Black, Sampit and Waccamaw Rivers and the shores of Winyah Bay produced almost all of the wealth of the Georgetown District. In 1850, there were fewer than one hundred plantations, with a total white population of two thousand, plus eighteen thousand black slaves. There was no manufacturing industry in the small town of Georgetown. All of the rice, lumber and naval stores produced by the plantations were sailed, rowed, poled or floated downstream to Georgetown in flat-bottomed cypress and pine boats, or lighters, until about 1825, when steamboats began to take over. Coastal schooners and sloops continued to transport rough rice to Charleston for processing. Although some coastal schooners sailed into Georgetown from northern cities to transport finished rice from the few large plantations that had their own mills, almost all international trade in rice was shipped from Charleston in larger sailing ships.

The brig *Globe*, whose homeport was Philadelphia, had sailed all over the world with freight and passengers during the 1830s and 1840s and had some involvement in the slave trade. She visited Georgetown several times to load lumber. On July 1, 1857, it was reported in the *Pee Dee Times* that Captain Roberts of the *Globe* had volunteered several members of his crew to help, with block and tackle, to raise a 1,400-pound bell to the top of the Market Tower on Front Street in Georgetown. The Market Tower was also used as a center for slave trading. Slaves were unloaded from ships that tied up to a wharf behind the Market Tower and led to an area at the base of the tower to be examined and sold to owners of rice plantations. The building, currently known as the clock tower, still stands.

The aristocratic rice planters of South Carolina had been made extremely wealthy by the labors of their slaves. Planters were able to entertain on a lavish scale. As an example, on April 21, 1819, President James Monroe was rowed up the Waccamaw River from Georgetown by eight liveried slaves in an elegant and profusely decorated plantation barge to a canal in front of Prospect Hill Plantation, where a red carpet was stretched from the landing to the plantation house.

The planters also held political power in the state. Poorer white farmers and middle-class tradesmen had almost no political power or say in the state government. Black slaves, of course, had no freedom or power and were completely dependent on the planters for their existence. The planters knew that their way of life would be destroyed if slavery were abolished. In the 1850s, as the institution of slavery was threatened by pressure on the federal government in Washington from the northern states, the rice planters of the Georgetown region of South Carolina led the way toward secession of the southern states to form a new country of slave-owning states. In 1860, they played a critical role in South Carolina's decision to become the first state to secede from the Union.

Soon after the Civil War started in Charleston in 1861, the Union navy sent ships to blockade the ports of Charleston and Georgetown. The Confederacy had no naval warships available to defend Georgetown at any time during the war, while Charleston was much better defended. The Union navy operated from its bases at Port Royal and Hilton Head Island, which it captured early during the war. On November 2, 1861, the U.S. transport ship *Governor*, carrying the U.S. Marine special "Amphibious Battalion" to Port Royal, sank off Georgetown, and the marines were transferred to another vessel.

To block the channel into Charleston Harbor, Admiral Dupont of the Union navy ordered that forty old whaling vessels be purchased in New England, loaded with granite stones, sailed to Charleston, stripped of their masts and sunk in the channel. This operation was known as the "Stone Fleet." It was not successful, however, because the weight of the stones pressed the ships deep into the mud and the channel was as deep as ever. One of the Stone Fleet whalers that was sunk was *Tenedos*, in which Herman Melville, author of *Moby Dick*, had once rounded Cape Horn and hunted sperm whales. He composed a poem lamenting the destruction of the whaling ships:

> *An old sailor's lament*
> *I have a feeling for those ships,*

Each worn and ancient one.
With great bluff bows, and broad in the beam
Ay, it was unkindly done.
But so they serve the Obsolete—
Even so, Stone Fleet.

To scuttle them—a pirate deed—
Sack them, and dismast,
They sunk so low, they died so hard,
But gurgling dropped at last.
Their ghosts in gales repeat
Woe's us, Stone Fleet!

Only one Union ship at a time guarded the entrance to Winyah Bay, usually the 116-foot, steam-powered, three-masted bark USS *Gem of the Sea.* Blockade runners, mostly steamers, were able to continue running in and out of Georgetown for most of the war. In December 1862, *Gem of the Sea* chased and crippled a British blockade runner, the schooner *Prince of Wales*, within sight of Georgetown Light. The *Prince of Wales* was run aground on North Island and set on fire. The largest blockade runner to enter Georgetown was the *Nashville*, a 216-foot converted passenger side-wheel steamer, which ran aground at the Winyah Bay entrance in 1862 but was finally able to make her way into Georgetown. The *Nashville* was the first ship to fly the Confederate flag in England. She eventually became the Confederate privateer *Rattlesnake* but was sunk by the Union ironclad *Montauk* in the Ogeechee River below Savannah in February 1863. Because Winyah Bay wasn't well guarded by Confederate forts, Union ships were able to steam up the bay to Georgetown and beyond. On May 28, 1862, Admiral Dupont reported to the United States secretary of the navy concerning Commander George Prentiss's incursion into Winyah Bay:

> *He stood up the bay to the city of Georgetown, entered Sampit Creek and steamed slowly along the wharves. Not being prepared to hold the place, Commander Prentiss did not land, knowing that there was a force of both cavalry and artillery in the town, and a contest might have involved the destruction of the city. He ascended the Waccamaw River, about ten miles above Georgetown, through a rich and beautiful country, meeting with no resistance. He took under his protection about eighty contrabands.*

During 1863 and 1864, there were fewer and fewer men available to defend Georgetown, and it became apparent that the South was losing the war. In February 1865, soon after the surrender of Charleston, three Union gunboats—the *Mingoe*, the *Nipsic* and the *Pawnee*—steamed up Winyah Bay, captured abandoned Confederate Battery White on the west bank of the bay and, days later, proceeded to Georgetown and accepted surrender of the town.

There was a Confederate shipbuilding facility at Mars Bluff Shipyard, almost one hundred miles up the Pee Dee River from Georgetown. There, the Confederacy constructed a well-armed 150-foot wooden gunboat, CSS *Pee Dee*, which was launched in December 1864. It was too late in the war for the vessel to move down the river and fight. In order for the *Pee Dee* not to fall into the hands of General Sherman, she was set on fire and blown up. The *Pee Dee*'s remains are currently being documented by archaeologists.

Command of the entire Union South Atlantic Blockading Squadron was in the hands of Admiral John Dahlgren, whose flagship was the wooden steamer *Harvest Moon*. In December 1864, the *Harvest Moon* was anchored south of Savannah, and General Sherman was aboard to discuss with Admiral Dahlgren the upcoming campaign to take Savannah. The assistant surgeon of the *Harvest Moon* reported in a letter home, "Sherman remained on board. He wears a seedy suit, slouch black hat, muddy boots with only one spur on, is 43 yr's old, a little sandy, prominent nose and looks as though he was a Brighton shoot-driver." By late February 1865, the *Harvest Moon* was

The only known photograph of the Union flagship *Harvest Moon*, taken in 1864. *Courtesy of Georgetown County Museum.*

anchored in Winyah Bay, near Battery White. On March 1, after inspecting the fortifications and making sure the town of Georgetown was secured, Admiral Dahlgren and the *Harvest Moon* weighed anchor and steamed toward the entrance. The *Harvest Moon* was a 193-foot side-wheeler, armed with a Parrott rifle and four howitzers. About three miles from Battery White, the *Harvest Moon* struck a floating mine, which blew a hole through the starboard quarter and tore away the main deck over it, causing the ship to sink in five minutes in two and a half fathoms. There were 108 men aboard the vessel, but the explosion killed only 1 man. According to Admiral Dahlgren's diary, "Suddenly, without warning came a crashing sound, a heavy shock, the partition between the cabin and wardroom was shattered and driven in towards me, while all loose articles in the cabin flew in different directions." For several days afterward, Union navy personnel stripped all valuable gear from the sunken vessel, and she was abandoned. The war ended in April 1865. The *Harvest Moon* still rests in the mud where she sank, her iron boiler protruding above low tide. The sinking of the *Harvest Moon* was the only loss of a flagship that the Union suffered during the Civil War.

CHAPTER 2

LUMBER SCHOONERS AND STEAMSHIPS

For ten years following the end of the Civil War, there was little but misery for the white and black people of Georgetown. The dominance of the rice planter culture came to an abrupt end with the emancipation of the more than ten thousand slaves of the region. The freed African Americans celebrated their freedom but had no means of earning a living, other than working for the "white man." There was almost no industry and few jobs. The freed slaves and poor whites did the most menial labor that was available and sharecropped or subsistence farmed and fished for food. Many of the planters, whose wealth had disappeared, could no longer pay taxes on their property, sold out at a loss and moved away. Ship traffic on Winyah Bay was brought almost to a standstill, until it slowly began to revive in the 1870s.

In 1874, Nathaniel Bishop, an early travel adventure writer from Massachusetts, made a journey in a fifty-eight-pound birch bark canoe, the *Maria Theresa*, from Quebec to the Gulf of Mexico. He paddled the entire distance. His route took him down the Waccamaw, Pee Dee and Black Rivers, through tannin-stained swamps and along isolated pine-forested riverbanks. As he paddled south from Conway, he passed ruined plantations and the shacks of the shingle and turpentine makers. He described steam sawmills and abandoned rice fields. He described cypress dugout canoes and big wooden lighters and flats piled high with cotton and naval stores. He spoke of once palatial plantation houses, taken over by Yankee owners, trying to grow rice with the labor of freed Negroes:

A steam tugboat and steamship on the Sampit River. By 1880, the Age of Steam was well underway. *Courtesy of Georgetown County Digital Library.*

Fine old mansions lined the river's banks, but the families had been so reduced by the ravages of war, that I saw refined ladies, who had been educated in the schools of Edinburgh, Scotland, overseeing the Negroes as they worked in the yards of the rice mills. "That lady's father," a gentleman said to me, "had owned three plantations, worth three million dollars, before the war. She now fights against misfortune, and will not give up. The Confederate war would not have lasted six months if it had not been for our women. They drove thousands of young men into the fight and now, having lost all, they go bravely to work, even taking the places of their old servants in their grand old homes. It's hard for them, though, I assure you."

He also described the poverty of blacks and whites and their mistrusting attitudes toward one another during Reconstruction. Bishop arrived in Georgetown in January 1875. He spent one night in Georgetown and was interviewed by the editors of all three newspapers. The people were very curious about his canoe and his long trip. The next day, Bishop paddled down the Sampit River and out Winyah Bay to Mosquito Creek; from there, he turned toward Charleston and eventually made his way to Florida.

One of the men who survived the Civil War and continued to do well was Henry Buck. His family were shipbuilders from Bucksport, Maine. Even before the Civil War, the Buck family had begun to import lumber from South Carolina for shipbuilding. Henry Buck decided to look for a suitable place

Painting of clipper ship *Henrietta* under full sail, by Charles Patterson. *Courtesy of Horry County Museum.*

in South Carolina to build ships and export lumber. He bought land about twenty miles up the Waccamaw River from Georgetown and established the town of Bucksville in 1830. Buck built several small ships along the shore of the Waccamaw River, proving to himself that it was more economical to build in Bucksville than in Maine. In 1874, he collaborated with Jonathan Nichols of Searsport, Maine, to build the largest sailing vessel ever constructed in South Carolina. Nichols imported skilled shipwrights from Maine and laid the keel for the *Henrietta*, a three-masted clipper ship 210 feet long, with a beam of 29 feet and a draft of 24 feet. She was launched in May 1875. Because of her deep draft and the limited depth of Winyah Bay, especially at the mouth, *Henrietta* was raised up on empty turpentine barrels, lashed to her sides, and towed to the ocean. The *Henrietta* sailed the seven seas for nearly two decades. In 1894, she was in Japan. At Yokahama, she loaded eight hundred tons of crockery and manganese ore and sailed for Kobe to complete her load before heading back to New York. She was caught in a typhoon and blown ashore and destroyed, although her crew was saved. Buck wanted to train local shipwrights and build more large ships in Bucksville, but the Maine shipbuilders rebelled and threatened not to buy lumber from Buck if he continued his shipbuilding operation in Bucksville. In 1883, Bucksville was a thriving community with a population of seven hundred. Following the Great Depression and the collapse of the lumber industry, Bucksville's name had been changed to Bucksport, but the town died and nothing is left.

During the 1870s, after the occupying Union forces had left and Reconstruction was fading, the South Carolina state government was back in the hands of white politicians. Rich Yankee industrialists had begun to take note of opportunities in the South. Some of them bought properties that had once been rice plantations, using the abandoned rice fields for duck hunting and the renovated plantation houses for winter getaways. Others studied how they could exploit the remaining natural resource of the region and bought timberland. Many of the longleaf forests had already been decimated by the naval stores industry. Ever since the early 1800s, pines had been slashed to collect gum, which was converted into turpentine, rosin and tar and shipped to Europe and other parts of the United States. Slashing of the pines made them more susceptible to diseases, insects and windstorms.

As the nineteenth century was drawing to a close, lumber barons from the East and Midwest selected Georgetown as one of the bases to cut the remainder of the South's virgin forests of pine and cypress, which they shipped as lumber to booming centers of commerce in the North. They bought thousands of acres of land for about a dollar an acre. They employed cheap Lowcountry labor to chop and saw the trees and haul the trunks to Georgetown's waterfront, where the trees were sawn into boards, beams, poles and railroad ties and loaded aboard steamers and topsail schooners headed for the ports of New York, Boston, Philadelphia and Baltimore. During the heyday year of 1905, 300,000 tons of lumber were shipped out of Georgetown. Mass exporting of lumber continued until the 1930s. Other products of the Lowcountry, including cotton, rice and naval stores, also continued to be shipped from Georgetown to the Northeast by schooner, but lumber dominated.

During the early 1900s, the Atlantic Coast Lumber Company mill in Georgetown was the largest lumber operation in the eastern United States, followed by Gardner and Lacey Lumber Company, Tyson Lumber Company and others. These companies, financed by northern banks and investors, built huge sawmills, wharves and railroad lines. They bought or leased steamships and sailing schooners to haul lumber and naval stores to the Northeast. They and the politicians of South Carolina successfully lobbied the federal government to deepen and improve the ship channel from Georgetown's Sampit River waterfront to the mouth of Winyah Bay. Between 1890 and 1905, massive stone jetties were constructed on both sides of the Winyah Bay entrance, and obstructions were removed to improve navigation on the Santee, Pee Dee, Waccamaw and Black Rivers, leading down to the port of Georgetown.

Georgetown was a bustling town during the late 1800s and early 1900s.

Lumber Schooners and Steamships

The Columbia *State* newspaper reported in May 1897:

> *Aboard the schooner* Warren B. Potter *the members of the Winyah Fire company yesterday gave their friends of Georgetown a most delightful excursion to North Island, distant, about 12 miles from the city on the Sampit.*
>
> *On the schooner all was life and merriment. The band played and the young folk danced to the music. Young America ran riot and played hide and seek from the very bottom of the schooner.*
>
> *On the way out refreshments of a substantial nature were served and the salt breeze only added to the zest in disposing of them. Soon after 9 o'clock North Island was reached. Here the young people broke up into two's and at convenient distances walked along the hard sandy beach. The moon shone bright and the night was such as lovers love. And judging from the interchange of tender looks, when the whistle of the* Congdon *sounded the recall, there were not a few of them.*

The *Georgetown Times* described the waterfront on a typical summer day in 1905:

> *Front Street all day long is filled with people, drays and wagons carrying merchandise; our merchants are busy; our banks are busy; our wholesale merchants are doing an immense business; our water front is alive with shipping of every description, as marked last week, when on one day, eleven large three and four masted schooners arrived, besides two steamships, two barges and the usual fleet of river steamers. There is hardly ten minutes any day but when your ear is greeted by the whistle of some ship, steamer or tug arriving or departing. It sounds sometimes as if you were in New York harbor.*

On April 9, 1905, the Columbia *State* newspaper reported the following thirty vessels loading during that week in Georgetown:

> *Steamer* Thistle, *loading for Santee: steamer* Eutaw, *loading for Pee Dee: steamer* Aragon, *loading for New York: steamer* Merchant, *loading for Pee Dee: schooner* Admiral, *loading for Nassau: steamship* Carib, *loading for New York: steamer* Planter, *loading for Charleston: steamer* Burroughs, *loading for Conway: schooner* Sylvia C. Hall, *loading for New York: steamer* Brunswick, *loading for Black River: steamer* Frank Sessoms, *loading for Bucksvill: schooner* Venus, *loading at Smith's Mills for New York: schooner* Charles Nobel Simmons, *loading for New York:*

The schooner *Ann Eliza*, unloading cargo in New York City, about 1880. In the background, the Brooklyn Bridge is under construction. Pitch, tar, turpentine, barrel staves, wood shingles and rice were some of the general cargoes shipped from Georgetown. *Courtesy of Georgetown County Digital Library.*

steamer William Elliott, *loading for Black River:* schooner Lizzie H. Patrick, *loading at Smith's Mills for Boston:* schooner Grace Seymour, *loading at A.C.L. Co. for New York:* schooner Massachusetts, *loading at A.C.L. Co. for New York:* schooner Gen. A. Ames, *loading at A.C.L. Co. for New York:* schooner Louis Bosset, *loading at A.C.L. Co. for New York:* schooner Benjamin Russell, *loading at Smith's Mills for Patchogue:* schooner Bayard Hopkins, *loading at Bucksport for Philadelphia:* schooner Chas. G. Endicott, *loading at A.C.L. Co. for New York:* schooner Richard Lithicum, *loading at Eddy Lake for Baltimore:* schooner R.R. Douglas, *loading at Winyah Lumber Co. for New Haven:* schooner Jesse W. Starr, *loading at Winyah Lumber Co. for New Haven:* schooner W.W. Potter, *loading at Winyah Lumber Co. for New Haven: Norwegian steamship* Emanuel, *loading for St. Johns, New Brunswick:* schooner Harold J. McCarty, *loading at Winyah Lumber Co. for New York:* schooner Wm. Lithicum, *loading at Gardner*

& Lacey Lumber Co. for Baltimore: schooner Lottie R. Russell, *loading at Winyah Lumber Co. for New Rochelle.*

In 1922, the four-masted schooner *Rassapeage* was tied up to a wharf on Georgetown's waterfront, loading lumber. Captain Olsen and his wife and daughter were aboard, and on the evening of October 18, as reported by the *Georgetown Times*, the Olsens

> *gave a party to their numerous friends, which will long be remembered by those who were present. The vessel's cabin was decorated with Japanese lanterns and plants which made the guests think they were in a hotel in the Tropics, rather than on board a vessel. Young people from the local community and the captains of other schooners in port enjoyed a collation and dancing until midnight.*

Investors or corporations outside South Carolina owned most of the schooners that visited Georgetown. One of the only locally owned schooners was the *Linah C. Kaminski*, owned by a group that included Heiman Kaminski. Kaminski was born in 1839 in Prussia, immigrated to America, fought for the Confederacy in the Civil War and built a hardware business in Georgetown that made him one of the wealthiest citizens of the town. The *Linah C. Kaminski* was named for his mother. Other owners of the schooner included members of the Buck family and several prominent citizens of Georgetown and Conway. The schooner was built by Goss Sawyer Shipyard in Bath, Maine, in 1882. She had three masts and was 134 feet long. She hauled as much as 300,000 board feet of lumber between Georgetown and northern ports. Her captain and part owner was S.E. Woodbury of Bucksville. During an early voyage of the *Kaminski* in July 1886 from New York to Georgetown, the daughter of the captain and a daughter of one of the Bucks traveled on the schooner and threw a bottle with a note over the side: "Becalmed near Frying Pan Shoals...alls well aboard the *Linah C. Kaminski*...please let the people at Georgetown and Bucksville know we are safe...signed Mollie C. Buck and Bessie G. Woodbury." The note was found and returned to the Kaminski family in 1976.

On March 27, 1887, the *New York Times* reported:

> *When in latitude 36 degrees 11 minutes and longitude 75 degrees 6 minutes, at 2 o'clock Tuesday morning, the schooner* Linah C. Kaminski, *bound from Georgetown, SC, for this port, was run into by the schooner,* Henry

Painting of the *Linah C. Kaminski* under sail, by E. Mikkelson, 1885. *Courtesy of Mr. and Mrs. Michael Prevost.*

Withington, *bound for Philadelphia. The crew of the* Kaminski *leaped to the deck of the* Withington, *leaving Capt. Woodbury and his wife alone on the wreck. The* Withington *soon drifted out of sight. On the following day the British ship* Dakota, *from Hamburg rescued the Captain and his wife and landed them at Baltimore. The abandoned vessel was picked up by a fishing vessel, which towed her to Sandy Hook, reaching there yesterday morning. Then a tug towed the prize into the Upper Bay. The agents, Hurlburt and Co., of South-street, say that she is now in the hands of the fishing crew, and will probably be repaired. She is 5 years old and measures 421 tons. H.H. Grant, of Georgetown, is her owner. The steamship* City of Puebla *made an unsuccessful attempt to tow the* Withington *to this port. She succeeded in reaching Philadelphia yesterday.*

The *Linah C. Kaminski* was off Cape Hatteras when the collision occurred. Captain Woodbury was quoted in the *Georgetown Enquirer* on March 30:

A letter from Capt. Woodbury at Baltimore gives full particulars of the disaster. He says he could have saved the vessel but for the cowardly desertion of his crew who, led by the mate, sprang aboard the other schooner immediately after the collision and resisted all his commands and efforts to induce them to remain. The Kaminski *lost her main and mizzenmasts*

and was stove in on the side near the waterline so that she began to fill.
Capt. Woodbury and his wife remained at or near the pumps the rest of the
night and until 8 AM on Wednesday, the 23rd.

The owners of the *Linah C. Kaminski* must have settled with the fishermen who claimed her as a prize, because she continued to sail into and out of Georgetown for many more years. It was reported in March 1914 that she was bound from Baltimore to Georgetown to pick up a load of lumber when she lost a topmast during a storm off the North Carolina coast but was able to reach port. However, on December 8, 1915, the *New York Maritime Register* reported, "A wireless from Miami Florida states that Spanish steamer *Conde Wilfredo*, from Galveston via Pensacola for Barcelona, and schooner *Linah C. Kaminski* from Newport News for Caibarien Cuba, were in collision yesterday in Lat 35 02, Long 74 22 (off Cape Hatteras), and the schooner sank; crew of latter rescued by steamer." The steel steamer *Conde Wilfredo* had collided with and sunk another Spanish freighter in 1913 off Gibraltar.

Well before Atlantic Coast Lumber Company moved into Georgetown and dominated the industry, there were many schooners loading lumber at smaller mills in Georgetown. In 1894, an internal commerce report for the U.S. Bureau of Statistics listed the three-masted schooners *B.I. Hazard* (305 T), *G.R. Congdon* (458 T), *Nellie Floyd* (457 T), *Graci N* (410 T), *D.K. Baker* (520 T), *Waccamaw* (458 T), *E.V. Glover* (288 T), *Linah Kaminski* (421 T) and *Hattie Buck* (233 T) as visiting Georgetown that year.

In 1884, the *Nellie Floyd* had been involved in a collision at night with another schooner, the *Royal Arch*. Both ships were seriously damaged, and the *Royal Arch* was found to be at fault. In 1889, the *Nellie Floyd* went aground at the north entrance to Winyah Bay while being towed out to sea by a tug. The tug's draft was too much to pull the schooner off. The shallower draft steamboat *Planter* came to the rescue after the *Nellie Floyd* jettisoned part of her cargo of rosin to lighten the ship. When the *Nellie Floyd* was pulled free and hoisted her sails, she let go of the towing hawser too soon and fouled a side wheel of the *Planter*. Once the hawser was cut out and both ships had docked in Georgetown, the two captains got into a dispute over how much should be paid to the *Planter* for salvage and the cost of the hawser. The dispute ended up as a court case, which the *Planter* won.

On December 24, 1892, the schooner *Eleanor McCoy* was in route from Georgetown to New York with a cargo of naval stores and cotton. Off Cape Hatteras, she was caught in a storm, her seams opened and she became waterlogged. The captain set fire to the ship, and the crew escaped in a tender to Topsail Inlet, North Carolina.

The three-masted, 137-foot *D.K. Baker* was built in 1882 at Port Jefferson, New York. It was reported that "her cabin appointments are unsurpassed by those of any vessel of the same class for beauty and elegance." In November 1898, the *D.K. Baker* was caught off the New Jersey coast in a snow- and windstorm. Although she shortened sail, her seams opened and she became waterlogged. Her crew members were freezing and held on for dear life. At 11:00 p.m., the ship was tossed on her beam-ends, with masts in the water. After a few minutes, her deck load broke loose and her mizzenmast and house were carried away. She righted herself, and the crew hung on for twenty-eight hours. Finally, during the next afternoon, the steamer *Falka* took the crew of the *D.K. Baker* on board. The *Baker* was abandoned.

A quarantine station was located on South Island, inside the Winyah Bay entrance, to inspect ships arriving from foreign ports. During 1892, the schooners *Pefetta, Beaver, Alferetta S. Snare, Edgar C. Ross, Z.S. Wallingford, Lena, Percy W. Schall, Annie F. Wahyah, Melvin, Edna and Emma, Minnie Bergen, B.I. Hazard, John H. Cannon, Charles C. Lister* and *Nellie Floyd* were inspected.

In 1899, the *Coast Pilot* and the chart *Approaches to Winyah Bay* indicated the wreck of a vessel, identified as the *Arethusa*, as a menace to navigation, with her boiler protruding. There were several *Arethusa*s in existence, but the most likely one was USS *Arethusa*, a 110-foot steamer built in 1864 and used as a collier during the Civil War. She was decommissioned in 1866 and sold, but her history after that time was not recorded.

Steamboats began hauling freight and passengers on the rivers above Georgetown long before the Civil War. The steamboats *Pee Dee, Maid of Orleans, Swan, Anson* and others hauled goods to Georgetown from as far up the Pee Dee River as Cheraw. Early steamboat travel on the rivers was not very dependable and was subject to groundings, snags and boiler explosions. Steamboats used inefficient single-expansion engines, requiring much coal or wood to fire their boilers. During the Civil War, most of the blockade runners and the Union ships that pursued them were propelled by steam. After the war, improvements were made, such as the triple-expansion steam engine, which made steamboats more efficient. The engines drove paddle wheels at the sides or stern of a steamboat. Before 1900, screw propellers began to replace paddle wheels. Later, oil replaced coal for fuel. Still later, gasoline and diesel internal combustion engines replaced steam engines for smaller ships and boats. Large ships progressed from multi-expansion steam engines to steam turbines. By the time of the steam turbine, almost no large wooden ships were being built.

Lumber Schooners and Steamships

The river steamers *Governor Safford*, *Planter*, *Maggie*, *F.G. Burroughs* and many others operated on the rivers and waterways near Georgetown in the early twentieth century. They made regularly scheduled trips from Georgetown up the Waccamaw River, stopping at landings to pick up and drop off passengers and freight. Some steamships made regular trips between Georgetown and Charleston and between Georgetown and other towns upstream, such as Conway, Marion and Cheraw. The *City of Columbia* provided steamer service from Georgetown to Columbia via the Santee and Congaree Rivers. River steamers disappeared as more rail lines were built and paved roads and bridges connected all towns. Larger steamships—operated by the Clyde Steamship Company, the Baltimore and Carolina Steamship Company and others—made regular passages between Georgetown and Wilmington, Norfolk, Baltimore, Philadelphia and New York. New York was a three-day steamer passage from Georgetown.

The industrial development of Georgetown's waterfront gave its citizens the unique opportunity to observe some of the last commercial sailing schooners in America. These magnificent three- and four-masted wooden ships sailed in and out of Georgetown Harbor by the dozens until a few years after World War I, when they would disappear forever. Largely due to the foresight of Georgetown's mayor, W.D. Morgan, many photographs of Georgetown's waterfront were taken between 1895 and 1910 and saved.

Over 1,500 sailing ships were built in the shipyards of Maine between 1890 and 1910. Many of them were built to be lumber schooners, sturdily constructed but without the fine finishes of a yacht. The largest schooners, huge five- and six-masters, had a draft of more than twenty feet, too much for the port of Georgetown. Most of those schooners were built to haul coal from ports in Virginia to the North. Many of the three- and four-masters regularly visited Georgetown to load lumber. Loading of lumber was done by hand by black stevedores, board by board, below deck and piled up on deck, requiring several days to complete. When the loading of a typical three- or four-masted topsail schooner was finished, the ship was towed or sailed away from the dock and guided along the narrow, twisting channel by a harbor pilot on board the ship to the Winyah Bay entrance and across the bar into the ocean. The ship's sails were set, and the pilot was taken back on board the pilot schooner. The lumber schooner got underway, riding the winds and the Gulf Stream northward, around Capes Fear and Hatteras, Graveyard of the Atlantic, toward one of the northern ports, a passage of over one thousand miles. The lumber on deck was lashed down with chains to keep the load from shifting as the ship rolled in heavy seas.

Above: The steamship *Governor Safford*. She carried passengers and freight from Georgetown up the Waccamaw River to Hagley Landing, where a train carried passengers to the beach at Pawleys Island. Atlantic Coast Lumber Co. built the rail line from Hagley Landing to Pawleys Island in 1902, but it was damaged by a hurricane in 1906 and was discontinued. *Courtesy of Georgetown County Digital Library.*

Below: The steamship *Burroughs* unloading freight at Wachesaw Landing on the Waccamaw River. *Courtesy of Georgetown County Digital Library.*

Lumber Schooners and Steamships

Top: Passengers embark on the riverboat *Elizabeth Ann* at Waverly Landing on the Waccamaw River. *Courtesy of Georgetown County Digital Library.*

Middle: A wooden barge, or lighter, under construction along the Sampit River. Tugboats pulled the loaded barges along the rivers and in Winyah Bay. *Courtesy of Georgetown County Digital Library.*

Bottom: A river steamer, loaded with cotton and wood shingles, a steamship loading lumber, a yacht's elegant launch and some fishing bateaus, all at Gardner & Lacey Lumber Co. wharf in Georgetown. *Courtesy of Georgetown County Digital Library.*

Above: Mules and wagons were used to transport freight in barrels to and from the Clyde Steamship Co. wharf in Georgetown. *Courtesy of Georgetown County Digital Library.*

Below: In 1896, Georgetonians celebrate completion of the Minim Canal, joining Winyah Bay to the Santee River, with an excursion to No. 10 steam dredge. *Courtesy of Georgetown County Digital Library.*

Above: A 1902 Georgetown parade up the Sampit River celebrating completion of a Winyah Bay jetty. Pictured are a boatload of surveyors, a boatload of ladies and a boat with a lady, a girl and a boy with a gun. *Courtesy of Georgetown County Digital Library.*

Below: Primitive United States Navy submarines visit Georgetown. *Courtesy of Prevost-Kaminski Collection.*

Above: An early seaplane gasses up along Front Street, attracting a crowd. *Courtesy of Prevost-Kaminski Collection.*

Below: A 1921 aerial view of Georgetown's waterfront, with two four-masted schooners tied up along the Sampit River. Goat Island was a peninsula then. *Courtesy of Georgetown County Digital Library.*

Lumber Schooners and Steamships

The heavily loaded ships usually made slow headway. They had no engine except for a steam-powered "donkey engine" that raised and lowered the big sails. The schooners sailed at all times of the year, with small crews of fewer than ten men. The crew was divided into two watches, each watch tending the ship for four hours and being off for four hours. Only the cook was relieved from standing watches. The duty watch had one man to steer the ship on a compass course, always watching the binnacle. Another man stood in the bow, keeping a constant lookout for other ships, especially at night. The captain or mate was the watch officer, checking to see that the ship carried the right amount of sail and that the course stayed true. They were always at the mercy of the winds and waves of summer storms and winter northeasters. The work was dangerous, and the pay for the crew was low. The ships had no wireless to communicate with the shore, and there was no Coast Guard to save a ship or her crew. An average passage of a sailing schooner to New York took about ten days.

Even today, almost everyone dreams of the romance of the sea and is fascinated by sights of tall masts, jutting bowsprits and webs of thick ropes rising from the decks of old wooden schooners. The deaths of those beautiful schooners and their clouds of canvas sails sadden many of us. We want to see them again, hear stories of their adventures and know what happened to them and their crews.

Fortunately, in addition to photographs of some of the schooners, there are records of the names and descriptions of schooners that entered and departed the lumber Port of Georgetown during the early 1900s. In the year 1900, there were thirty different three- and four-masted schooners, with the names *Cherubim*, *Nellie Ford*, *Wilson & Hunting*, *Oliver Schofield*, *Bayard Hopkins* (lost off Norfolk in January 1919), *Ida C. Schoolcraft* (lost off Core Bank in July 1902), *John I. Snow* (lost off Portsmouth in January 1907), *George R. Congdon* (wrecked off Hatteras in February 1901), *Rebecca R. Douglas* (stranded off the Maine coast in December 1916) and many others.

In December 1900, the *Oliver Schofield*, a three-masted schooner, was on her way to New York with a cargo of lumber and was caught in a sixty-mile-an-hour gale off the coast of New Jersey. She was too close to shore and couldn't work her way off, so she dropped her anchors. They didn't hold, and the *Schofield* was driven broadside and grounded 350 feet from the beach. The men from a lifesaving station fired a line to the schooner, and a breeches buoy was rigged to bring Captain Sprague and his crew to shore. The *New York Times* reported, "Scarcely had Captain Sprague made the trip along the line when the foremast rolled out, carrying with it both topmasts and the other sticks. An hour later both the other masts went, and the hull began to pound on the beach. She is rapidly going to pieces, and the beach is strewn with the lumber which formed her cargo."

In 1904, more than sixty schooners of over 100 feet in length cleared the Port of Georgetown. They included the 180-foot *Nathan Lawrence*, which sailed from Georgetown for Bridgeport in September 1904, carrying a load of lumber. The *New York Times* reported on September 18:

The third shipwrecked crew to be landed in Wilmington since the disastrous hurricane of Tuesday and Wednesday came up to the city yesterday. The rescued men were Capt EW Barlow and seven men, who were taken from the wreck of the schooner Nathan Lawrence *in the Gulf Stream, off Cape Romain.*

The Nathan Lawrence *sailed from Georgetown, SC last Monday. The hurricane struck the ship at 6 PM Tuesday and carried away every sail, though snugly furled around the booms. Huge seas boarded the ship, swept both lifeboats away, the forward house, the midships house, and all the water tanks and belongings of the crew. In the midst of the awful sea, Tuesday, at midnight, the ship sprang a leak, and filled in thirty minutes. Nothing was left above water but the after house, and on to this the crew lashed themselves and waited for daylight.*

At the break of day, Wednesday, the schooner D.J. Sawyer *sighted the wreck and bore down on it. The sea was too rough all day to allow a boat to be launched, but at 5:30 o'clock in the evening a boat was put over and all hands were saved.*

The rescuing schooner herself had suffered from the storm, having lost her jib boom, mainsail and two headsails.

During that same hurricane of September 1904, the schooner *Emily F. Northam* had sailed from Georgetown, and the *Times* reported:

The steamer Chatham *from Savannah, today, reports that last Thursday night, off the South Carolina coast, the three master schooner* Emily F. Northam *of Philadelphia was seen ablaze amidships.*

A strong wind carried showers of sparks from the burning vessel. Her decks were awash, her masts standing, and her burgee still flying, but all her gaffs and booms were gone with the exception of the main gaff, and her yawl boat was missing.

Captain Hudgins of the Chatham *got as close as safety would permit, but could discover no signs of life aboard, and he believes the crew got away in her yawl. The schooner was lumber laden and may have become water logged in the cyclone Thursday night, the crew setting fire to her before leaving.*

The schooner *Wilson & Hunting* survived the storm of September 1904 but was run down and sunk by the big U.S. Navy supply ship *Calgoa*, with the loss of four of her crew, on a clear night in November 1904. The *Wilson & Hunting* was on her way from Norfolk to New York with a load of wood piling stacked on her deck. The 145-foot, three-masted schooner was under full sail and showing her proper navigation lights when the *Calgoa* loomed up from behind and struck her at full speed, almost cutting the schooner in half. The *Times* reported:

When the crash came, Captain Walton, his wife and all the crew were on deck. The Captain and his wife were standing on the deckhouse, and the big steel prow cut into the schooner within a few feet of them. It is believed that, when the Calgoa *backed off and the vessel went down with the Captain, his wife and the two lost sailors, they were buried under the big deck load of piling and drowned or knocked senseless.*

The survivors are of the opinion that Captain Walton lost his life trying to save his wife. They say he could have clambered on board of the supply ship, as they did but the vessel backed off before he could get his wife on board or do anything on her behalf. Captain Walton and his wife lived at Tuckerton, N.J. He came from a family of seafaring men, his father Captain Robert I. Walton, Sr. being now in command of the De Mory Gray, *of which the younger man was formerly Master. His brother is Captain of the* Henry P. Haven. *Another brother of the dead man, Clarence Walton, committed suicide on board the* Wilson & Hunting *in March last, when he was her captain.*

Captain Robert I. Walton, Jr. saved his wife from death on a former occasion while he was in command of the De Mory Gray. *The incident happened very near the spot on which the collision of Wednesday occurred. The vessel was caught in a terrific storm on March 15, 1903, and while her decks were awash and the boat in a sinking condition, Captain Walton lashed his wife to the top of the mainmast and he and his crew managed to keep the vessel afloat until she was taken in tow by a passing vessel and brought to this port. Mrs. Walton was nearly frozen to death, but she persisted in accompanying her husband on his voyages, and the sailors say that they were much devoted to each other. Captain Walton was thirty-five years old, and his wife five years his junior.*

Other schooners that cleared Georgetown in 1904 included the *Jesse Barlow*, which went aground in June 1904 off Fire Island, New York. She was pounded hard, and her cargo of deck lumber went overboard. She could not be refloated, and the U.S. Army Corps of Engineers finally removed her sunken remains in 1907.

The 180-foot *Eliza J. Pendleton*, which was carrying a load of lumber from Georgetown to Bridgeport, was wrecked in a gale off the coast of New Jersey in February 1906. The crew of eight men was saved.

The *Everett Webster*, with a crew of seven, sailing to Philadelphia with lumber in March 1907, was caught in a gale and wrecked off Cape Hatteras. The crew held on to the submerged wreck for several days and were picked up by a French bark and taken to Rouen, France. They returned to the United States in April.

The *William H. Skinner* left Georgetown in February 1908. A day later, a gale shredded her sails and filled her with water. After three days, her mainmast went overboard and the schooner capsized. The men lashed themselves to the wooden hull, which drifted east for six days. The men were on the verge of starvation when they were discovered near the Azores Islands by a steamer traveling from Galveston to Belfast. They were transferred to a Cunard Line steamer, taken to England and finally returned to the United States.

The three-masted schooner *Golden Ball* was launched in Kennebunkport, Maine, in 1890 and was a regular visitor to Georgetown. On January 28, 1909, she was stranded in a gale on Egg Rock, three miles south of the lifeboat station at Great Wass Island, Maine. The schooner's crew was picked up and brought to the station. Attempts were made to float the *Golden Ball* on the next day's high tide, but she was fast on the rocks and went to pieces.

The *Thomas G. Smith* went down off Core Bank in April 1910.

The *Sarah D. Fell* was headed for Boston in August 1910 with a load of lumber when she was hit by a hurricane and sunk. Her crew was saved.

In a September 1911 storm, the schooner *Malcolm B. Savory* sank off Georgetown with nothing but her spars showing above water. During the same storm, the three-masted schooner *Fortuna* lost her mast and all rigging but was saved and towed into Georgetown by the U.S. revenue cutter *Seminole*.

The *Lottie R. Russell* was bound for New York with a cargo of lumber in September 1913 when she was dismasted by a storm and capsized off Cape Henry. The crew was taken off, and the hulk drifted north for one thousand miles and was towed into Halifax, Nova Scotia.

Lumber Schooners and Steamships

In 1914, a Georgetown newspaper described the arrival of two 170-foot, four-masted schooners, the *John Bossert* and *Louis Bossert*, being towed up the channel in tandem to load lumber. In February 1916, the *John Bossert*, hauling lumber from Georgetown to New York, caught fire off Sandy Hook, New Jersey, and burned to the waterline, although the crew was saved. The *Louis Bossert* had a close call in April 1907, when she was stranded off Nags Head at night. The lifesavers from Nags Head station took the crew of ten, including the captain, his wife and daughter, off the ship, and the ship was eventually refloated.

The *John Paul* was carrying a load of granite from Maine in January 1914 when she and her crew were caught in a gale and lost off Nantucket Sound.

An attempt was made to improve the efficiency of schooner transportation by creating schooner barges, bulky wooden schooners with three or four short masts, with sails to be used only in an emergency. Two or more loaded schooner barges were towed to their destination by an oceangoing tug. They were not safe ships in a storm. During the hurricane of July 1916, the tugboat *Wellington* was towing two 110-foot wooden schooner barges, the *South West* and the *North West*. They were located fifty miles west-southwest of Frying Pan Lightship when winds and waves became so severe that the *Wellington* cut loose the two schooner barges. They were blown onto the shoals off Cape Romain. The *South West* and her crew of eight men were lost. The crew of the *North West* was saved by the heroics of the Cape Romain lighthouse keeper, August Wichmann.

The 140-foot *Charlotte D. Sibley* was discovered by the newly launched navy ship SS *New Mexico* in derelict condition off Norfolk in February 1919, so she tested out her guns by sinking the hulk.

The four-masted *Chas G. Endicott* was on her way from New York to Cuba in February 1921 and apparently struck a mine near Cuba and sank. Later in the year, the captain and the owner of the schooner were indicted and jailed for conspiring to scuttle the ship to collect insurance.

In October 1921, the almost new four-masted schooner *Phoebe Crosby*, on her way from Providence, Rhode Island, to load at Tyson Lumber in Georgetown, ran into the Winyah Bay south jetty. The Columbia *State* newspaper reported:

> *Captain Small, in explanation of the accident which proved fatal to the ship, states that a sudden squall caught his vessel, a swift cross current contributing, and she was swung hard against the rocks, her stern receiving such severe damage that she sank, with only the stern and the cabin remaining above water. Capt. E.F. Redell, the light keeper, with the tender*

Palmetto, witnessed the catastrophe and rendered immediate assistance under circumstances requiring great courage and coolness. He afterwards stood by, and for days was the means of communication and transportation between the land and the distressed master and crew, who refused to leave the ship.

Joseph Conrad said, "The Sea has never been friendly to man. At most it has been the accomplice of human restlessness."

Although coastal schooners of the late 1800s and early 1900s were not built to make regular ocean crossings or to have very long lives, some of them did make Atlantic crossings and some did last beyond the average schooner lifespan of twelve years. One of these ships was the four-masted schooner *Clara Davis*, which sometimes loaded lumber in Georgetown. She was built in Mystic, Connecticut, in 1905. She was a lumber schooner for much longer than most of her contemporaries. Late in her life, she crossed the Atlantic and engaged in the Baltic lumber trade. Her name had been changed to *Martha of Parnu* when she was grounded, fully laden, off the Swedish coast in January 1938. She was towed to Copenhagen, where she was dismantled and her wooden hull was broken up.

The four-masted schooner *Charles Wittemore* was built at the same time and place as the *Clara Davis*. She visited Georgetown twice in the year 1916.

A wreck of a schooner towed into Georgetown. A number of ships and boats have run into the jetties and been lost. *Courtesy of Prevost-Kaminski Collection.*

Steamer tug *Congdon*, tied up in front of the Tarbox House. The *Congdon* towed schooners from the early 1900s until there were no schooners. *Courtesy of the Tarbox Collection.*

In 1918, she was commissioned by the U.S. Navy as a decoy ship. She was accompanied on her passages by a U.S. Navy submarine in attempts to destroy German submarines. The *Wittemore* survived the war and remained in merchant service until 1921, when she was abandoned at sea.

In 1899, Charles R. Flint, a New York financier known on Wall Street as the "father of trusts," put together a syndicate to form the Atlantic Coast Lumber (ACL) Company of Georgetown, South Carolina. Soon, ACL grew to become the largest lumbering operation on the eastern seaboard. ACL bought thousands of acres of dirt-cheap South Carolina timberland, clear cut the timber, hauled the logs on their own railroads to the mill, cut the logs into boards and shipped billions of board feet of lumber to the northeastern states. By 1900, most lumber was being shipped by steamer, and the days of lumber schooners were numbered. Lumber steamers, usually built of steel, could carry two or three times as much lumber and could make three or four times as many trips during the same period as sailing schooners, but steamers were expensive to build and required much coal to power them. By 1901, Atlantic Coast Lumber had leased two large steamers to haul lumber.

Mr. Flint, however, was also a sportsman and sailing enthusiast and had been part owner of the 1894 America's Cup winner *Vigilant*. He and his associates decided, whether from nostalgia or for business reasons, to build their own schooner to haul lumber. In 1902, ACL contracted with the well-respected William Rogers Shipyard of Bath, Maine, to build a four-masted, 185-foot, six-hundred-ton schooner. William Rogers was known as the dean of Bath shipbuilders. A Bath newspaper reported that this schooner, the 100th built by Rogers, "would be the handsomest craft of her size to engage in the lumber business."

Left: The four-masted topsail schooner *Clara Davis* loads lumber in Georgetown. *Courtesy of Georgetown County Digital Library.*

Below: Vast piles of lumber at Atlantic Coast Lumber Company. A small part of it is being loaded aboard the three-masted schooner *Warren B. Potter*. *Courtesy of Georgetown County Digital Library.*

Above: A three-masted schooner unloads granite stones to be used for the Winyah Bay entrance jetties. *Courtesy of Georgetown County Digital Library.*

Right: Three three-masted schooners fly flags from the peaks of their topsail masts during a visit to Georgetown by President Grover Cleveland. *Courtesy of Georgetown County Digital Library.*

Above: The three-masted schooner in the foreground flies her spanker and mizzen topsail. In the background are two three-masted schooners. The waterfront of Georgetown is crowded with railroad cars, logs, piles of lumber and work barges loading stone. *Courtesy of Georgetown County Digital Library.*

Below: A three-masted schooner with a long jib boom and a shiny dark hull loading lumber in Georgetown. *Courtesy of Georgetown County Digital Library.*

Above: Six three-masted schooners tied up along Georgetown's waterfront to load lumber in 1905. *Courtesy of Georgetown County Digital Library.*

Below: Two four-masted schooners. The log raft in the foreground awaits a tow to the sawmill. *Courtesy of Georgetown County Digital Library.*

Above: A two-masted schooner, loaded with lumber, leaves the Sampit River under full sail. *Courtesy of Georgetown County Digital Library.*

Below: A three-masted barque is pushed up windless Winyah Bay by a steam tug. *Courtesy of Prevost-Kaminski Collection.*

Lumber Schooners and Steamships

Above: The four-masted schooner *City of Georgetown* arrives in Georgetown in 1902 after her maiden voyage from Bath, Maine. *Courtesy of Georgetown County Digital Library.*

Below: Georgetown's citizens visit the four-masted schooner *City of Georgetown* after her maiden voyage. *Courtesy of Georgetown County Digital Library.*

It usually took five to six months, from keel laying to launching, to complete a typical four-masted schooner. The keel for the *City of Georgetown* was laid along the shore of the Kennebec River in Bath, Maine, on a cold March day in 1902. The keel was assembled from several long and heavy oak timbers, stretching out for 160 feet. Next, ribs called frames were built up from several curved oak timbers, one frame at a time on a flat platform, and stood up to form the skeleton of the hull. A massive keelson was constructed inside the keel to form the backbone of the structure. The inside hard pine planking, called ceilings, were fastened to the frames using iron bolts, drift pins and hardwood treenails, stiffening the frame. After deck beams and all other framing was completed, exterior pine planking was fitted and fastened to the outside of the frames and then caulked with cotton and oakum and sealed with pitch. The decks were laid and the forward and aft deckhouses constructed so that the ship was weather tight. By that time, four 90-foot-long, eight-sided Oregon pine masts had arrived from the West Coast on three flatbed railroad cars linked together. The masts, jib boom and all other spars were shaped and fitted with hardware. All of the standing rigging, running rigging and the topmast were attached to each mast before they were raised. The donkey engine, supplied by Hyde Machinery Company of Bath, was installed. A lifting frame, called a sheer-leg, extended 70 feet above the deck of the schooner and was used to raise each mast to a vertical position and lower it to the mast step. This was the most exciting operation of building the ship, except for her launching. Power from the donkey engine lifted each fifteen-ton mast into place. Joinerwork, painting, rigging, piping and machinery proceeded to completion. Two three-thousand-pound anchors were placed on board. The sails were bent on, and the ship was ready for launching. The *City of Georgetown* was launched on November 1, 1902.

Her captain was A.J. Slocum. Abram Jones Slocum was born at sea near the Azores aboard his father's whaling ship, the *Saratoga*, on September 14, 1861. The *Saratoga* had set sail from New Bedford, Massachusetts, in 1856 on a four-year whaling expedition. Captain Frederick Slocum's wife, Lydia Jones Slocum, accompanied him and gave birth to twins, Abram and a sister. By the time the *Saratoga* returned to New Bedford, the Civil War had started, but Frederick Slocum continued to hunt whales, commanding the ships *Swallow* and *Starlight*. By that time, the market for whale oil had disappeared, having been replaced by petroleum. In 1871, Frederick Slocum retired and built a house on the island of Cuttyhunk. There, his wife gave birth to more children, including a son, Frederick, who would one day become a well-known astrophysicist. Frederick said, "From childhood the boys were taught the ways of boats and the sea." Abram's father died in 1885. Abram followed in his father's footsteps, serving as mate and captain of several vessels. In June 1898, he married Lillian Remine. They had one child, Marjorie Lillian, born in February 1901 in Somerville, Massachusetts.

Homeport for the *City of Georgetown* was New Bedford. Captain Slocum, who had been with the ship since the beginning of construction, and his crew made the ship's maiden voyage to Georgetown, arriving on December 3, 1902. "She received a big ovation from our city. The whistles blew and the bell rang, announcing her arrival. She was towed up from the bar by the tug *Congdon*."

From that time on and for more than ten years, Captain Slocum and his seven-man crew made passages, as often as once every two months, from ACL's loading docks in Georgetown to New York, Philadelphia, Boston and other New England ports, loaded above and below decks with about 600,000 board feet of lumber. The *City of Georgetown* then sailed south with a cargo of coal or salt and returned to Georgetown to load lumber. Little is known about Captain Slocum's personal life during that period. His wife and child continued to live in Massachusetts. Captains had, by far, the best living conditions aboard their ships, with a private bath and the cook providing them with the best food available. Existing account books of Kaminski Hardware Store of Georgetown from the early 1900s show occasional purchases of oakum, lamp wicks, paint and rope by the schooner *City of Georgetown*, authorized by the captain. He was a master mariner and a hell of a sea captain to avoid the fate of so many other wrecked sailing vessels, fighting storms and currents off Cape Hatteras and Diamond Shoals, at all times of the year. However, the *City of Georgetown* had a close call in September 1906, when she was caught in a gale off Cape Hatteras. Bound from Georgetown for Philadelphia with a cargo of lumber, her sails were blown out, her seams opened and she would have sunk except for the buoyancy of her cargo. The German tramp steamer *Carl Menzel*, headed for Russia, towed the *City of Georgetown* to a wharf in Norfolk and claimed salvage. The owners of the *City of Georgetown* settled the claim and had the schooner repaired and put back into service.

Much less is known about A. J. Slocum than about his famous but unrelated namesake, the single-handed circumnavigator Joshua Slocum, who said in his autobiography, "If any Slocum should be found not seafaring, he will show at least an inclination to whittle models of boats and contemplate voyages." The famous Joshua Slocum did pass through Georgetown on one occasion. After a series of adventures, a mutiny, a murder, some sinkings and the death of his first wife, Captain Joshua Slocum was stranded in 1888

Above: Cape Romain Lighthouse, where Joshua Slocum visited on the *Liberdade* in 1888. *Courtesy of Prevost-Kaminski Collection.*

Below: The side-wheel steamship *Planter* hauling cotton and passengers. The *Planter* gave Joshua Slocum's *Liberdade* a tow to Georgetown. *Courtesy of Georgetown County Digital Library.*

along the coast of Brazil with no money, a second wife and two children. With his own hands, he built a thirty-five-foot wooden sailing canoe with a junk rig, at a total cost of $110, and named her *Liberdade*. He and his wife and children set sail from Brazil and touched land at Barbados and Puerto Rico before sailing through Cape Romain inlet and anchoring behind Cape Romain Light on October 28, 1888.

Slocum was befriended by a local farmer, who gave him supplies and guided him toward Winyah Bay by way of inland creeks. The steamer *Planter*, passing by on her way from Charleston to Georgetown, offered Slocum a tow, which he accepted. This was the second of two steamships named *Planter* that carried cotton and passengers between Charleston and Georgetown. The second *Planter* was also the one that rescued the *Nellie Floyd* and was involved in a dispute with her captain, as described previously. The first *Planter* was built in 1860 and served as a Confederate transport and dispatch vessel until May 13, 1862, when Robert Smalls, her African American pilot, steamed out of the port of Charleston at night and turned the ship over to Union forces. The *Planter* returned to commercial service after the war but was lost at sea off Cape Romain in 1876.

When Slocum was towed into Winyah Bay by the second *Planter*, he was informed that he would have to clear customs, particularly because he had a coconut plant on board. The customs agent didn't arrive when he had promised, so Slocum set sail for the mouth of Winyah Bay and into the ocean to New River, North Carolina, and up the Potomac River to Washington, D.C. This voyage occurred several years before he began the first ever single-handed sailing voyage around the world in *Spray* in 1895.

The three- and four-masted coastal lumber schooners of the late 1800s and early 1900s were able to be competitive with steamships in part because they could operate with such small crews, which was made possible only because of their use of steam-powered donkey engines to turn the winches to raise and lower their big sails. The schooners' gaff-rigged sails required much less manpower aloft than square-rigged ships, where many hands were needed along the yardarms to handle sails. As ocean-crossing square-riggers and schooners were replaced by steamships, the quality and experience of sailors decreased. The captain and possibly the mate were the only ones on board a lumber schooner who knew enough about navigation to take sextant shots and work out calculations of latitude and longitude positions as the ship worked its way north or south, out of sight of land. Many of the sailors who served on lumber schooners had never been to sea on a sailing ship before, and some had never been to sea at all.

Most sailors preferred to serve on steamers because the work was easier. Sailing skills were being lost, and a schooner captain was lucky to find some old Norwegian sea dog in a New York bar who would agree to sign on to make a passage for the low wages he could pay. These sailors were never a dependable lot. As Samuel Johnson said, before 1800, "no man will be a sailor who has contrivance enough to get himself into a jail; for being in a ship is being in a jail, with the chance of being drowned...A man in a jail has more room, better food and commonly better company." At least the voyages in a coastal schooner were shorter than those on a clipper ship or a whaler. It is not known what problems Slocum encountered in acquiring and keeping dependable crews over a period of ten years. The ship's log went down with the ship in 1913.

Just after midnight on the cold, clear night of February 3, 1913, the four-hundred-foot, six-thousand-ton ocean liner *Prinz Oskar* collided with the *City of Georgetown*. The *City of Georgetown* was reaching to the south under full sail before a brisk east wind. She was on route from New York to Savannah with a cargo of salt and was off the southern tip of New Jersey, near the mouth of Delaware Bay. Her running lights were burning, and her crew was aware that a large steamer was approaching in the distance, from the direction of Delaware Bay. The one-thousand-passenger liner *Prinz Oskar* had left Philadelphia with a crew of one hundred but only six first-class passengers and thirty steerage passengers on board. She was owned by the Hamburg American Line and was on her way to Hamburg, Germany. The port pilot had just left the *Prinz Oskar*, and her officers were plotting her course for Hamburg. The *Prinz Oskar* was proceeding at full speed. Captain Slocum, who had completed the 2000 to 2400 watch, had gone below to his cabin, and his mate had charge of the watch. His crew consisted of seven men beside himself—Johnson the mate, Peterson the engineer, a steward and four able seamen. One seaman, Malmberg, was a lookout in the bow, and another, Olsen, was at the wheel as steersman.

The sailor on watch in the *Prinz Oskar*'s crow's-nest, eighty feet above the water, sighted a white light, which he thought was coming from a lightship a few miles east of them. But as the *Prinz Oskar* moved away from the direction of the lightship, it soon became evident that the light was from a ship. The watch reported the light to the bridge but received no reply. When the light was closer, the watch could see that an electric torch was being shined on the sails of a large sailing vessel. By the time the steamer's captain and officers noticed the white light and the green starboard navigation light of the *City of Georgetown*, the *Prinz Oskar* was too close to avoid a collision.

Lumber Schooners and Steamships

The *New York Times* reported:

> *In desperation the crew of the* City of Georgetown *tried to change direction but it was too late. Her bowsprit stretched out like a battering ram and struck the* Prinz Oskar. *Through the steel plates the bowsprit jammed its way, carrying both of the schooner's anchors and the* Prinz Oskar*'s huge port anchor ten feet into the forecastle. Sailors asleep in their berths were jerked to the floor amid shattered fittings and ice.*
>
> *The impact was so powerful that the steel liner was rocked. Passengers were thrown from their bunks. At the same time the four masts of the schooner snapped off and fell to the deck, with the mass of spars, sails and rigging. For a few minutes the wooden ship and the liner were locked fast by the bowsprit. Then, the big twin screws of the liner's engines reversed and pulled her free, jerking the schooner's bowsprit from its fastenings. As the steamer backed, the schooner immediately settled at the bow and started to sink.*

With the decks in a tangle and the vessel rapidly sinking, Captain Slocum and his crew had a hard time saving themselves. Slocum and two of his men were able to launch a dory. They began to row away from the schooner just as she was sinking. The other four men had jumped overboard and were still in the water. The last sailor overboard had been knocked from his bunk in the foc'sle by the collision, had grabbed his sea coat and run up the slanted deck, toward the stern, leaping over the tangled rigging. With the stern facing almost straight upward, he climbed over a rail and dove toward the dory. The dory was almost swamped by the suction of the sinking vessel. The men in the dory tried to row toward the others, who were trying to swim to the dory. The men in the water managed to cling to a piece of floating wreckage but were being swirled deeper and deeper into the maelstrom caused by the rapidly sinking stern of the schooner. Captain Slocum stood up in the bow of the dory and threw a line toward the other men, who grabbed onto it and were able to pull themselves to the side of the dory. The dory rowed out of the whirlpool just as the stern of the schooner disappeared below the swirling water. Lifeboats from the liner helped bring the crew of the *City of Georgetown* on board the *Prinz Oskar*. Many of the passengers of the *Prinz Oskar* had panicked and fled to the icy decks but were finally calmed by the stewards. The *Prinz Oskar* returned to Philadelphia for repairs. The captain and crew of the *City of Georgetown* were returned to port.

The *Prinz Oskar* continued to ferry passengers between Philadelphia and Hamburg until the start of World War I, when she was confiscated by the

United States government, renamed the *Orion* and converted into a troop ship. She was scrapped in 1929.

In 1914, Abram J. Slocum filed a civil suit, on behalf of the owners of the *City of Georgetown* and the International Salt Company, against the owners of the *Prinz Oskar*. The *Prinz Oskar*'s German officers were found guilty of negligence in the collision, despite their claim that they had done nothing wrong, that the captain and men of the *City of Georgetown* were lying about their navigation lights and that they, as German officers, were superior in education and training to the crew of the schooner. The District Court of Pennsylvania ruled that the *City of Georgetown* had shown the correct navigation lights, continued her course and speed and had right of way over a ship under power:

> *The steamship is clearly at fault for failure to observe Sailing Rule 20 by keeping out of the way of the schooner; for failure to have a competent lookout properly stationed; for failure on the part of the officers in charge of the* Prinz Oskar *to observe with a degree of attention which would have apprised them of the presence of the schooner, and for failure to act promptly in reversing the engines when the collision might have been avoided.*

After the *City of Georgetown* went down, A.J. Slocum continued to command other sailing ships. Later, according to his brother Frederick, "Abram Slocum was lost at sea with his schooner and all hands, off the coast of Virginia-Carolina northward bound. No report of the disaster ever came."

Today, the few remaining bones of the *City of Georgetown* lie on the bottom of the Atlantic Ocean, one hundred feet below the surface and a few miles off the entrance to Delaware Bay. Divers say that nothing, not even the "cabin of ash and red cherry, finished so as to leave in tact the beauty of her natural wood," protrudes more than five feet above the ocean floor.

The year 1913 was not a good one for Atlantic Coast Lumber Company. In addition to losing the *City of Georgetown*, there was a disastrous fire at the lumberyard that destroyed many of its buildings and much stored lumber. The yard was rebuilt, and the lumbering operation continued throughout World War I and up until the Great Depression. The company closed down in 1932. "Then, one year there were no more logs to make lumber," said Ernest Hemingway in his short story "The End of Something."

Georgetown harbor pilots are skilled seamen who know the Winyah Bay ship channel and who have guided ships in and out of Georgetown for many years. Members of the seagoing Skinner family were Georgetown harbor pilots for several generations. Captain Bill Skinner started his career operating an oceangoing tugboat, pulling one-hundred-foot wooden schooner barges, with masts and sails, loaded with lumber from Brunswick, Georgia, to New York. He was the first Georgetown harbor pilot after International Paper Company started using the port to haul construction materials in 1936. One of his first jobs as harbor pilot was to pilot the four-masted schooner *Anna R. Heidritter* up Winyah Bay to Georgetown to load lumber. The *Heidritter* came to her end in 1942, off Ocracoke Island. Her seventy-three-year-old Captain Coleman was running the schooner closer to Cape Hatteras than usual to avoid a U-boat attack, and the *Heidritter* grounded on the beach at Ocracoke and broke up.

When Bill Skinner retired, he gave his pilot boat, *Kermath*, to his nephew, Wright Skinner Sr., who was a fisherman and charter boat captain, as well as harbor pilot. He owned the *Lillian Skinner*. When he retired in 1972, he turned the job of harbor pilot over to his son, Wright Skinner Jr., who was already his assistant. Wright Skinner Jr. was a shrimper as well as harbor pilot and operated a sixty-five-foot steel vessel. During a stormy night in February 1988, Wright Skinner Jr., age fifty-nine, guided a ship through Winyah Bay and into the Atlantic. While reboarding the pilot boat, he was washed overboard and drowned.

Between 1879 and 1921, over 1,500 three-masted schooners were built in the United States, as well as 531 four-masters, 45 five-masters and 10 six-masters. World War I created a demand for many new ships, both steel and wooden hulls, and even some new four-, five- and six-masted sailing schooners. Scores of them were built in the shipyards of Maine and other locations along the Atlantic, Gulf and West Coasts. The need for ships was so great that in 1914 the U.S. government paid to have the abandoned and sunken four-masted schooner *Venita* raised from the bottom of the Sampit River so that it could be salvaged and used during World War I. A few schooners survived the Great Depression, continuing to haul lumber, phosphate, salt and coal until the beginning of World War II. Among them were two four-masters that visited Georgetown many times after World War I to load lumber.

The *Purnell T. White* was launched in August 1917 at Sharptown, Maryland, on the Nanticoke River. She was a four-masted topsail schooner, 197 feet long with a 38-foot beam and a draft of 14 feet. Her gross tonnage was 751. During the rest of the war, she made passages to Africa and Brazil. After 1919, almost all of her passages were along the East Coast, as far north as Nova Scotia and as far south as Trinidad. Her first visit to Georgetown was in 1921 to load lumber for New York. She made a few more appearances

Looking aft as the four-masted schooner *Purnell T. White* approaches Georgetown in 1933. The stack is the donkey engine exhaust. This would be one of her last voyages. *Courtesy of Georgetown County Digital Library.*

in Georgetown during the 1920s, but her regular visits started in November 1928. After that, the *Purnell T. White* loaded lumber in Georgetown and unloaded in Baltimore or New York almost every two months until January 1934. During that passage, from Georgetown to New York, she was caught in a gale off Cape Fear, North Carolina, and her sails were shredded. A U.S. Coast Guard vessel came to her assistance and took her in tow, despite terrible weather. Off Cape Henry, the weather deteriorated further, and the *Purnell T. White* started to sink. The seven-man crew requested to be taken aboard the U.S. Coast Guard vessel *Mendota*. The sea was so rough that three of her Norwegian crew and seventy-four-year-old Captain Nicklas were drowned. The hulk of the *Purnell T. White* was towed into Norfolk, unloaded, stripped and sent to a bone yard near Baltimore, where her hulk rotted away over the next forty years. There is an excellent account of her history in *Sea, Sails and Shipwreck* by Robert H. Burgess.

Captain Nicklas had for many years been a regular visitor to Georgetown, which he considered his second home. Charles Nicklas was born in Germany in 1864 and had come to the United States when he was nineteen years old, seeking gold. When that treasure eluded him, he turned to the sea. He sailed on vessels of the coffee fleet, trading between Baltimore and Brazil. He eventually gained command of coasting schooners and became master of the *Purnell T. White* in the mid-1920s. In 1927, he tried to retire to a farm he had purchased in Maryland, but three months later, he was back at sea. The voyage in 1934 was to be his last before retiring to his farm.

The other four-masted schooner that was built during World War I and often visited Georgetown was the *Albert F. Paul.* The *Purnell T. White* completed a passage from New York to Georgetown on October 28, 1933,

Looking aft from the crosstrees of the *Purnell T. White*. On the right, the four-masted schooner *Albert F. Paul's* deck is loaded with lumber. The schooners are tied up at Tyson Lumber Company's wharf. *Courtesy of Georgetown County Digital Library.*

and tied up alongside the *Albert F. Paul*, which was loading lumber at the Tyson Lumber Company dock in Georgetown. The loading was finished on November 1, and the *Paul* swapped places with the *White* so she could load. The *Paul* was scheduled to depart for New York early during the following week, so the crews of both ships decided to have a social gathering on the Saturday before she left. James McCullough, who was serving as a seaman aboard the *White*, gives this account:

> *The crews of both schooners drew money and it wasn't long before the South Carolina corn liquor was flowing freely. At first the party was quite sociable; singing started, later to be followed by a fight and some knife play. No one was seriously injured but the* **Paul**'s *forecastle was pretty much of a wreck. By ten o'clock Sunday morning the money and liquor were all gone, most of the crew stretched out, and the rest of Sunday was quiet and peaceful.*

The *Albert F. Paul* was launched at Milford, Delaware, in 1917. She was of similar size and configuration to the *Purnell T. White*. She continued to make passages as a lumber schooner until the beginning of World War II. On May 18, 1933, the *Albert F. Paul* was anchored off a Georgetown sea buoy, awaiting a tug and the pilot boat. James McCullough was on board and reported:

> *Fresh breeze but moderating, called all hands at 5 AM. Coffee. Hove in some chain. Put a harbor furl on the jibs. Sea going down. The tugboat* W.H. Andrews *came out about 10 AM. The pilot, Captain Porter, came aboard. Passed the hawser to the tugboat, hove in the anchor and got underway. Set the main, mizzen and forestaysail. The tug could not keep ahead of the vessel. Hauled down the forestaysail and dropped the peak of the mizzen. Fifteen miles up Winyah Bay to Georgetown. About two miles below the town lowered the main and mizzen sails and tied them up. Unhooked the jib sheets and coiled them down close up in the bow to be out of the way. Unshackled the lower fore, main and mizzen sheet blocks, pulled them up two blocks, and coiled the sheets over the ends of the booms. Hove the main and mizzen booms up well clear of the deck to be out of the way when loading. Put shores under the boom jaws and unhooked the throat halyards, which will be used in loading. When the vessel was abreast of the town the tug blew three long blasts of the whistle to let the townspeople know a vessel had arrived in town.*
>
> *Tied up to the Atlantic Coast Lumber Company dock about 3 PM. Cleared up the deck, swept down and knocked off. The captain's family, friends, and relatives of the crew were down on the dock to meet the ship. The arrival of the* Albert F. Paul *seems to be an important event.*

The schooner would load over 500,000 board feet of lumber before returning to New York.

There exists a list of all the voyages made by the *Albert F. Paul* from 1917 through the end of 1941. Most of the items on that list are not particularly interesting, such as "Sailed for Georgetown January 30, Arrived at Georgetown February 27, Sailed for New York March 18." However, one entry that aroused curiosity was "October 31, 1927. Arrived at Georgetown. Captain Jones shot in knee November 8 and leg taken off November 9. Capt Charles Nicklas in charge, November 16."

Laura Jones Meyer of Georgetown was the youngest daughter of Captain Robert O. Jones, master of the schooner *Albert F. Paul* from 1924 through 1941. In 2011, Mrs. Meyer and her brother, Albert F. Paul Jones, who was named after the ship and grew up aboard her, represented the last living connection between Georgetown and the lumber schooners that sailed from Winyah Bay. They knew the story of their father and the rest of the family.

Robert Jones was born in North Wales in 1896. He ran away to sea on a square-rigger in 1914 and was a member of the crew of a British bark that was sunk by a German submarine in 1916. For a short time he crewed on steamers. In March 1924, he was mate on a schooner that went aground off Cape Hatteras and was a total loss. In August 1924, he took over as captain of the *Albert F. Paul* and was one of the youngest East Coast lumber schooner captains in the fleet. During one of his first trips to Georgetown to load lumber, he met his future wife, Maud Ainsworth, who lived in Georgetown. They were married in December 1924, and Mrs. Jones moved aboard the *Albert F. Paul*. Their first daughter was born in a West Indies port less than a year later. Mrs. Jones made all of the schooner's voyages, raising two daughters and a son aboard ship until the oldest daughter reached school age. Then, she and the children lived ashore in Georgetown, except for summers, when the whole family lived aboard.

Albert Jones told me that while the *Paul* was becalmed, which was often, he and his mother would fish with hand lines from the stern. On one occasion, his mother's hand line became wrapped around her leg while a big shark was on the other end of the line. One of the ship's crew ran to her and cut the line just before she was pulled overboard.

When the ship was loaded with lumber, the distance from the deck to the water, the freeboard, was less than six feet, and flying fish often jumped onto the deck. The ship's pet dog, which loved to chase flying fish, once fell overboard. A crewman tied a rope around his waist and dove in to save the dog.

When the *Paul* was in Georgetown, she tied up either in front of the Kaminski House or at the Tyson Lumber Company wharf at the end of Cannon Street. While ashore, Captain Jones and his family lived in their house on Front Street. The captain's two beautiful German shepherds stayed on the ship for most of their time in port but found their way to the house whenever they managed to escape. A sad memory of Albert Jones was when one of the shepherds had a leash around its neck when it jumped over the side of the ship trying to go home.

During his tenure as captain of the *Paul*, Jones had many adventures, some shared by his family and others not. In 1926, the *Paul* was detained in Maine for a month when the U.S. Coast Guard discovered that the crew was smuggling liquor. In 1927, while the ship was loading lumber in Georgetown, Robert Jones lost his leg in a hunting accident and was relieved for a short time. He stumped about on a cork leg for the rest of his career. In 1932, the

Paul was caught in a storm, and Captain Jones suffered a concussion and temporary blindness. Later that year, the *Paul* began to leak so badly she had to be towed into port. In 1933, the *Paul* ran through a hurricane and suffered minor damage. In 1939, she was washed aground off the Rhode Island coast and towed off. On one occasion, a storm came up suddenly as the *Paul* was entering Winyah Bay. Her sails were up, and there was no way a tug could be of help. Captain Jones steered the *Paul* all the way up Winyah Bay and managed to sail her right alongside the Atlantic Lumber wharf, with only a little damage to the pier, a feat never before or after accomplished by such a large sailing ship with no auxiliary power. Captain Jones retired from the *Paul* when she was sold in 1941. He was mate on steamers during World War II. He died in Georgetown in 1963.

The last captain of the *Albert F. Paul* was William Martino. On March 15, 1942, the *Paul* was on her way from Turks Island to Baltimore with a cargo of salt when she was spotted by the German submarine U-332. The submarine's captain considered using his deck gun to destroy the schooner, but the sea was rough, so he fired a torpedo. The first torpedo passed under the bowsprit, but the second one struck under the third mast, and the *Albert F. Paul* sank immediately. The schooner's crew of eight men was lost.

Another lumber schooner that visited Georgetown several times during the 1930s and was lost to a German torpedo during World War II was the *Doris Hamlin*. She was a two-hundred-foot, four-masted schooner built in Maine in 1919 and owned by the Vane Brothers of Baltimore. She carried pulpwood, lumber, coal and logwood all up and down the East Coast. She was sold by Vane in 1939 and sunk by a submarine in 1940.

The wooden four-master that outlived all the others was the *Annie C. Ross*. She was 176 by 38 by 14 feet and was built in 1917 in Bath, Maine, by Percy and Small, the shipyard that built several of the world's largest schooners, including the largest wooden sailing vessel ever built, the six-masted *Wyoming*, measuring 350 by 50 by 30 feet. The *Wyoming*'s hull construction consumed 2,400 tons of yellow pine, some of which might have been shipped from Georgetown. The *Annie C. Ross* was successful in the lumber trade in the 1920s and '30s. She was one of the first schooners to have a gasoline internal combustion donkey engine rather than a steam engine for hoisting sails and anchors and driving pumps. The *Annie C. Ross* visited Georgetown several times to load lumber. She participated in one of the last bull markets for schooners, carrying building materials to Miami for the Florida land boom of the 1920s. She was laid up in New York in 1940 and never went to sea again. In 1954, she was bought by a scouting organization that intended to

The bow of the *Albert F. Paul* is in the foreground. In the background is the barque *Sea Cloud*, 1939. *Courtesy of Mrs. Laura Meyer.*

restore her. However, it wasn't able to raise enough money, and the *Annie C. Ross* sank at her moorings at Glen Cove, Long Island, in 1955.

As a teenager, author Frederick Kaiser crewed on the *Annie C. Ross* under Captain Zuljevic. In 1937, the *Annie C. Ross* was anchored off Georgetown Light awaiting a tug. When the tug didn't arrive, the *Ross* was towed up Winyah Bay by two shrimp boats and again anchored off Frasers Point, awaiting space at the Tyson Lumber Company. The steamship *Vamar* was at Tyson loading lumber while the *Ross* was anchored.

The *Vamar*, although not a wooden ship, had an interesting history. Built in 1919 in Middleboro, England, with the name *Kilmarnock*, she was 170 by 30 by 16 feet, with a triple expansion steam engine. Later, she was bought and renamed *Chelsea*. In 1928, she was confiscated in England for smuggling whiskey, and Rear Admiral Richard C. Byrd bought her to be a supply ship

Above: The four-masted schooner *Annie C. Ross* loads lumber in Georgetown in the late 1930s. *Courtesy of Prevost-Kaminski Collection.*

Left: The *Annie C. Ross* under sail. *Courtesy of Georgetown Digital Library.*

for his Antarctic exploration expedition. He renamed the steamer after his mother, *Eleanor Bolling*. She became the first iron ship to be used in polar ice pack waters since the *Titanic* sank in 1912. Because of the *Eleanor Bolling's* hull shape, she was known by her crew as "Rolling Bolling." The *Eleanor Bolling* carried in her hold the airplanes that Byrd used to fly over the South Pole. The *Bolling* returned to New York and was greeted with much fanfare, but Byrd considered her unseaworthy for a second expedition and sold her in 1930. Vamar Shipping Company bought the steamer in 1933 and renamed her *Vamar*. She hauled freight until 1942, when she sank, overloaded, off Port St. Joe, Florida.

Fred Kaiser described the arrival of the *Annie C. Ross* in Georgetown:

> *When the* Annie C. Ross *was finally moved (again by midget flotilla) to her loading berth, it was an undeniably lively and noisome affair. First, the starboard anchor was dropped to swing on, along which our various small-fry helpers hastened to rearrange themselves to nudge us alongside. The whole town was on hand to watch the maneuver, hear the captain's accented invectives, and applaud when we were fast to the surviving portion of the decrepit wharf.*
>
> *On Sunday, after they had been to church, and attracted by the tall masts of the* Ross, *half the population of Georgetown County would visit the ship. The boys aboard were tour guides and the captain was a genial and proud host. At such times, however, Old Charlie, our shellback bosun, could be a problem. Usually hung over and quite out of sorts, he could be counted on to provide a dramatic appearance in his hasty trips from the foc'sle door to the scuppers.*

The last, largest and most luxurious schooner to have an impact on Georgetown wasn't wooden and wasn't a working sailing ship. In April 1931, the 359-foot, four-masted steel barque *Hussar V* was launched in the Krupp Shipyard in Kiel, Germany. She had four diesel auxiliary engines and a giant stabilizer and could travel twenty thousand miles without refueling. The ship had forty-two tons of refrigeration equipment, capable of storing vast quantities of food for extended voyages. The owners were Edward Hutton, founder of E.F. Hutton, and his wife, Marjorie Merriweather Post, heiress to the cereal fortune of Post Toasties and Raisin Bran. Equipped with a magnificent owner's suite and six guest suites, the owners cruised the world, accompanied by their little daughter, Nedinia, who would one day become actress Dina Merrill. After three-month cruises during the years 1932 through 1934, the couple decided to divorce. For some reason, while

Marjorie Merriweather Post's four-masted barque, *Sea Cloud*, drying her sails in Georgetown in 1935. *Courtesy of Georgetown County Digital Library.*

the divorce proceedings were going through the courts, the *Hussar V* was laid up in the port of Georgetown, South Carolina. In the end, Marjorie Merriweather Post received custody of *Hussar V* and immediately changed her name to *Sea Cloud*. She soon married third husband Joseph Davis. In March 1935, the newlyweds took their honeymoon in the West Indies aboard *Sea Cloud*. Of the seventy-five-member crew, seventeen were from Georgetown. Returning from their honeymoon, Joseph Davis was appointed ambassador to Russia. *Sea Cloud* sailed for Leningrad, where she became a floating diplomatic palace. At the beginning of World War II, Marjorie loaned *Sea Cloud* to the war effort. Her masts were removed, and she was painted gray. She returned to Georgetown and served as a U.S. Coast Guard cutter until the end of the war. After the war, *Sea Cloud* was given back to Marjorie Post, but she eventually sold her to dictator Trujillo of the Dominican Republic, who renamed her *Angelina*. Trujillo was assassinated in 1961. German businessmen eventually bought and restored *Sea Cloud*. Today, she serves as a luxury cruise ship for wealthy vacationers.

Georgetown always had a problem with the depth of the Winyah Bay ship channel, even after extensive dredging and the construction of massive stone jetties at the mouth of the bay at the turn of the century. In 1905, the ship channel had been deepened to eighteen feet, still not deep enough for the largest steamers to get into port to load lumber. About 1950, to accommodate the ships serving International Paper Company, the channel was deepened to twenty-seven feet, and a portion of the channel was relocated, with annual dredging necessary to maintain that depth. At first, spoil from dredging was deposited along the shorelines of the bay. Since this was not a satisfactory procedure, diked spoil areas were created to hold the pumped spoil. Winyah Bay is fed by eighteen thousand square miles of watershed, forming hundreds of miles of rivers that empty into the bay. By the end of the 1950s, all of the rivers emptying into Winyah Bay had been dammed far upstream to form recreational lakes and to produce hydroelectric power. The dams' effect on the flow of water into Winyah Bay also affected silting of the bay. Maintaining a depth of twenty-seven feet, which still wasn't deep enough for big ships, became a major dredging problem.

The commercial importance of the Port of Georgetown declined after the Great Depression and the end of the lumber boom. The opening of International Paper Company's huge mill in 1937 provided a temporary revival of port activity. For several years, tugboats towed wooden or steel barges, piled high with pulpwood logs cut from fast-growing pine trees, up the Sampit River to the mill. However, by the 1980s, the use of barges to haul pulpwood logs had been abandoned and replaced by trucks. International Paper Company shipped thousands of rolls of kraft paper to Europe from the Port of Georgetown. During one month in 1967, twenty-four ships visited Georgetown, and the average for that year was fourteen ships per month. During the 1980s, use of the port declined as bigger and bigger ships were built to haul cargo in containers. The relatively shallow Georgetown ship channel was used less and less for commercial shipping.

As shipping decreased, so did the demand for tugboats. In 1905, there were more than twenty tugboats that operated in Winyah Bay. One of the tugs that served Winyah Bay was the *Georgetown*, built in 1901. Her name was changed to the *Helen McAllister*, and she is currently displayed at the South Street Seaport Museum in New York City. In 2011, only one tug remained tied up in Georgetown Harbor.

CHAPTER 3

FISHING BOATS

The waters of Winyah Bay and the ocean and rivers nearby have always been fertile grounds for fishermen. Hundreds of wooden sailing sloops, schooners and periaguas fished in and around Winyah Bay from colonial times until the early 1900s, when steam and internal combustion engines replaced sails. Revolutionary War general and North Island summer resident Peter Horry stated in his diary of 1812 that his slave, Scipio, used hook and line from the boat and in the surf to catch whiting, croakers and catfish. Horry said, "Having now a suitable Boat and Seine, I hope never to want fish of all Kinds."

Some fishermen sailed offshore, overnight, as far and farther out than the Gulf Stream, which is more than fifty miles from shore. They returned days later with their catches to sell at fish houses along Georgetown's waterfront. There, fish and shrimp were bought and sold or iced down and shipped to other cities. Small boats brought their catches of bass, flounder, pan fish, crabs and oysters from Winyah Bay to the fish markets. At one time, there was an oyster factory at the end of Cannon Street, where lines of black ladies shucked oysters, which were sealed in jars or steamed and canned. For over two hundred years, the fishermen of Winyah Bay sailed, rowed or powered their wooden fishing boats in and out from the busy docks along Front Street at all times of the year. Winyah Bay has always been a rough and treacherous body of water in bad weather and has claimed—and still claims—the lives of fishermen who venture out when winds are too strong.

Every spring, commercial shad fishermen in small boats placed long gill nets in the bay or near the mouths of inlets. The nets drifted and caught

Boy, fish and man. *Courtesy of Georgetown County Digital Library.*

shad that were starting toward the rivers to spawn. Later in the spring, stake row nets, sturdy poles supporting gill nets, were pushed into the mud of Winyah Bay to catch sturgeon for their valuable caviar roe. Boats owned by Rene Cathou and Herbert Tarbox unloaded shad and sturgeon fish at Cathou's Fish House, where they were packed in barrels and shipped out by truck and rail. The roe was cut out, salted, packed in jars and sold locally or shipped to New York City and other destinations. A 1965 letter to Rene Cathou from Meadowbrook, Pennsylvania, reads, "I should like very much to order some of your caviar. 12 lbs. In ½ pt. jars. It is truly excellent and gives many of my friends a great deal of pleasure. It was $7 per pound, when last I bought it, but I shall wait for a bill. Very sincerely, Anne Rowland."

The days of plentiful and inexpensive local seafood may be over. Fishing for sturgeon was outlawed many years ago. Seasons for commercial and recreational fishing for many species have been shortened. Stocks of fish, oysters, crabs and almost all other marine life have been depleted by overfishing, by pollution from the rivers and the paper mill and by decreased marine habitat. There are restrictions on the methods of fishing and the length of seasons, and limits have been placed on numbers and sizes of fish that can be taken. Still, some of the best-tasting seafood in America is caught in or near Winyah Bay.

Fishing Boats

Rene Yves Cathou Sr. left France on a sailing ship as a young man in the 1880s and found a commercial fishing job in the northeastern United States. He came to Charleston after the earthquake of 1886 and was told that the best fishing was in Georgetown. He moved to Georgetown and fished for McDonald and Company, which built the fish house at the end of St. James Street about 1898. By 1905, Rene Sr. was operating the trawler *Lottie C.*, named after his first wife. The *Lottie C.* capsized and was lost, along with her crew, while shrimping between the north jetty and Murrells Inlet in 1957. Rene Sr. took over the fishing business from McDonald and Company in 1908 and started Cathou's Fish House. Rene Sr. married Mary, and they had two sons, Rene Jr. and Bubba Joe. When the sons grew up, the business became R.Y. Cathou and Sons.

In 1945, R.Y. Cathou and Sons bought the vessel *Maude & Mable*, a forty-five-foot wooden trawler, built in 1937 in New Jersey. When Rene Sr. died, Bubba Joe and Rene Jr. took over the business. They owned and fished many wooden boats. The *Mary P. Cathou* was named for their mother. The *Rene Y. Cathou* was named for their father. She met her end, piled up on the jetties. Rene and Bubba Joe built the forty-eight-foot *Prodigal Son* in 1948. She was fitted with three small gasoline engines so she had less draft and could trawl in Winyah Bay's shallow Mother Norten Shoals, where no other boat could fish. The *Joey Cathou* was built in the 1950s, named for Bubba Joe's son. Bubba Joe died in 1972, leaving Rene as sole owner of the business.

Rene was a great storyteller and a character not to be forgotten. On a typical winter day, Rene unlocked the door of the dilapidated and unpainted cypress board and batten fish house and fired up a potbellied heater in the middle of the main room. Soon he would be joined by an array of local fishermen, live-aboard boat people and other regulars, all huddled around the heater, swapping the latest rumors and fish stories. The entire inside of the building was cluttered with leftover paint cans and piles of wood and rusty metal, leaning against bulkheads and hanging overhead. There was a fish-cleaning sink, a big walk-in cooler room for storing iced-down fish and a room full of tools and equipment for repairing boats. A rough stair led up to a long, low space that ran the length of the building, where there were racks for building and repairing nets and more room for storing boat stuff. Rene had a separate office with a battered old desk, a heavy iron safe and boxes and barrels of miscellaneous metal parts and tools. The office walls were plastered with old photographs, faded advertisements and out-of-date calendars.

Above: Shrimp trawlers *Mary P. Cathou*, *Rene Y. Cathou* and *Maude & Mable* at Cathou's wharf. The two-story structure in the left background is the dredge *Barlow*. The two-story house in the right background is the Tarbox House, built in 1765. *Courtesy of Mr. Joe Cathou.*

Below: The shrimp trawler *Capt Andrew* was built in Georgetown in the 1950s and was still part of a dwindling shrimp fleet in 2011. *Photo by the author.*

Fishing Boats

Above: A fishing schooner's captain and crew of fourteen return to a Georgetown wharf. Fish were caught with hand lines from dories, seen stacked on the foredeck of the schooner. *Courtesy of Georgetown County Digital Library.*

Below: The fishing schooners *Robert* and *Carr* tied up at Cathou's wharf. *Courtesy of Georgetown County Digital Library, Caines Collection.*

Left: The menhaden trawler *Montauk* and another trawler are tied up alongside two steam tugs. A menhaden factory was located up the Sampit River. *Courtesy of Prevost-Kaminski Collection.*

Below: Rene Cathou strides down the wharf at Cathou's Fish House and marine railway. *Courtesy of Georgetown County Digital Library, Caines Collection.*

Fishing Boats

It might have been during one of those sessions around Rene's potbellied stove that the story of Fair-Haired Annie was first told. It seems that, sometime around the turn of the century, there was a lighthouse keeper at Georgetown Light who lived out there on North Island with his little daughter, Annie. One day, he had to go to Georgetown to buy supplies, so he and his beloved daughter got into the dory and rowed with the tide across Winyah Bay and into town. By the time he was ready to go back and light the great lantern before darkness fell, the wind had picked up. He rowed as hard as he could. Waves splashed into the boat, soaking him and Annie, huddled against him in the stern. When they were only a few hundred yards from the shore of North Island, the little boat was swamped and capsized. The keeper tied his daughter to his back and swam toward the shore. Overcome by shock and exhaustion, he didn't remember crawling ashore. Many hours later, he awoke to find his drowned daughter still strapped to his back. From that day on, sailors reported stories of a sweet blond child appearing on their boats, usually on calm sunny days, pointing to the bay and pleading, "Go back!" Always, her entreaties preceded violent, unanticipated storms.

During the early days of Cathou's Fish House, there was no marine railway. Rene used Brightman's railway, at the Sampit River end of Cannon Street, to pull his fishing boats out of the water when they needed bottom work. One day, Rene told Brightman he needed to use his railway to pull a boat, and Brightman told Rene that he couldn't do it that day because he had promised his wife he would take her for a drive in the country. That was the day that Rene decided to build his own marine railway. At first, Cathou's railway had no power winch. Rene would hook a cable to the floating boat's cradle and the other end to his truck and pull the cradle and boat up the railway. When the truck reached a certain spot in the middle of Front Street, a block away, Rene knew the boat was clear of the water. Finally, when Panther Johnson's Boatyard closed down, Rene confiscated the old pull motor from Panther's.

Rene continued the business of fishing for shad and sturgeon and buying fish and shrimp from other fishermen, like Roy and Jerry Caines and Ronnie Campbell. Rene finally retired from the fish business in the mid-1980s but continued to run the marine railway. He died in 2000 at the age of eighty-eight. Bubba Joe's son, Joe, inherited Cathou's Fish House. Ronnie Campbell, who had worked for Rene and who had bought Rene's trawler, *Prodigal Son*, in 1978, took over the marine railway. He currently lives in a houseboat next to the wharf, surrounded by a great variety of stray cats, ducks, pelicans and an ancient one-eyed bulldog, Precious.

A fleet of steam-powered menhaden schooners worked off the Georgetown coast for many years, bringing their catches to a factory up the Sampit River. In September 1914, the Columbia *State* newspaper reported:

> *The steam fishing schooner* **A.M. Hathaway**, *217 tons, Capt. Luce, Greenport, N.Y., is hard ashore at North Inlet, Winyah Bay, and she will probably leave her bones there. She is broadside on the beach, drawing 11 feet and with a scant six feet around her at high spring tide.*
>
> *She is practically full of sand and water, her siphons and pumps are clogged with sand and there is scarcely one chance in a hundred that she will ever float again.*
>
> *The* Hathaway *carried a crew of 24. All were saved.*

Since the early 1900s, during the summer months, a fleet of wooden shrimp boats has left the docks of Georgetown and trawled in the Atlantic, catching thousands, even millions, of pounds of shrimp. Up until the end of the 1990s, big shrimp were plentiful and profits were high. In 1997, the shrimp fleet of Georgetown harvested 2.7 million pounds of shrimp and fish. Thirty women worked on either side of a conveyor at Independent Seafood, heading and grading shrimp. Shrimp and fish were iced down and stored or trucked to restaurants and markets all over the Southeast, and even as far away as the Fulton Fish Market in New York.

Many of the larger wooden trawlers were built with oak ribs and Douglas fir or southern pine planking in St. Augustine, Florida, between the end of World War II and the mid-1970s. The *Capt. Andrew* was the only large shrimp boat that was built in Georgetown and was still shrimping in 2011. Another fleet of shrimp trawlers operated out of nearby McClellanville. In 2011, the last sizeable commercial wooden boats that remained in Georgetown were a few old diesel-powered shrimp trawlers. There have been fewer of them every year, as the catches were smaller, foreign farm-grown shrimp caused prices to go down, fuel became more expensive, hulls rotted and weren't repaired and fiberglass and steel trawlers took over. The remaining wooden trawlers were tied up along the Front Street waterfront, awaiting the beginning of shrimp season. A few others were tied up to the derelict lumber piers of Goat Island, across the Sampit River from Front Street, and would probably never fish again.

The Tarbox family has been in the fishing business for three generations. Herbert Tarbox operated the business before his son, Glennie. Independent Seafood is at the Sampit River end of Cannon Street, where Tyson Lumber

Fishing Boats

Company's wharf had been and where Brightman's marine railway was located until 1945. About 1939, the Tarbox family owned and fished the wooden smack *Stella*. She had a Norwegian crew who first arrived in Georgetown on some ship from abroad and never left. In the seafood buying and selling business, they had contact with many wooden boats. The *Naomi* was a wooden buy boat, a type of Chesapeake Bay shallow draft fishing boat with a cabin in the stern, which moved down to Winyah Bay and was converted into a shrimp trawler. The *Lydia* was a sailboat that was converted into a trawler. Currently, Independent Seafood and Stormy Seas Seafood are the only remaining seafood markets along the waterfront of Georgetown.

CHAPTER 4

YACHTS AND PLEASURE BOATS

Wealthy men and women have always owned boats for their own pleasure. Almost all of the men who bought the old rice plantations and those who profited from the lumber boom owned their own yachts, power cruisers, skiffs, launches or bateaus, and almost all of them were built of wood until the 1960s, when fiberglass started to become popular. Bernard Baruch ferried his guests, including Prime Minister Winston Churchill and President Franklin Roosevelt, from Georgetown to his estate at Hobcaw aboard the wooden launch *Sea Dog*. Baruch was once fined by the U.S. Coast Guard for not having a life preserver in his motorboat, *Chick*. President Grover Cleveland was hunting ducks from a wooden bateau when he became stuck in the marsh mud of Winyah Bay near Hobcaw. The Yawkeys took the Detroit Tiger and Boston Red Sox baseball players, including Hall of Famers Ty Cobb and Lefty Grove, fishing and hunting aboard the power cruiser *Elise*. The DuPonts, Huntingtons, Emersons and Vanderbilts all had their own yachts tied up along riverbanks near Winyah Bay.

The Santee Gun Club, a group of forty wealthy northeastern and South Carolina sportsmen, reorganized itself in 1900 and leased the two Murphy Islands, south of the Santee River, for their annual duck hunting. A 1904 marine survey showed that the club boat, *Gardenia*, an old stern-wheel steamboat, acquired in 1899, was " a mere shell, bored through and through by teredos," so another boat was required. The new club houseboat, *Happy Days*, was built in New York in 1905. She was seventy feet long with an eighteen-foot beam and drew two feet, four inches. She was designed to have a gasoline engine, but the club decided at the last minute to make her a wood-burning steamboat, requiring a very large and heavy boiler in the stern. Henry Carter stated in his *Early History of the Santee Club*:

> *The result was the boat was so low in the water that the deck at the stern only cleared the water by six inches. It took four months to bring the boat from New York to Santee as it was not safe to proceed except in a calm. The boat was satisfactory after arrival at Santee, but was very expensive to run as she required a duplicate set of house servants in addition to the crew.*

The houseboat *Happy Days*, "elegantly finished inside and provided with every convenience," made frequent trips through Winyah Bay to Georgetown until 1925, when she was sold and replaced by an Elco Boat Company cabin cruiser.

Bootlegging, rumrunning, white lightning stills, homemade corn liquor and avoiding taxes on whiskey have always been part of the scene in port towns where sailors get liberty. From 1893 until 1907, the State of South Carolina dispensed its whiskey in distinctive bottles to make sure that taxes were collected. Federal Prohibition, from 1919 until 1933, was largely ignored along the coast of South Carolina. Small vessels landed cargoes of illegal liquor in the coves and creeks along the coast near Georgetown. Occasionally, the vessels failed to find safe harbor. Such was the case with a schooner found beached and burned on Debordieu Beach in 1932, with seventy-five cases of whiskey still on board. Some of the coasting schooners hid illegal liquor from the West Indies in their bilges and passed it to selected distributors. The U.S. Coast Guard caught the crew of the *Albert F. Paul* transporting illegal alcohol in 1926. In 1924, a Hollywood silent movie, *Pied Piper Malone*, was made in Georgetown. In the movie, the ship's captain has a weakness for liquor, which he finds at the Blind Tiger, a speakeasy in the local barbershop.

After World War II, the chartering of sport fishing boats became popular in Georgetown. One of the first charter boat captains was Sam Crayton, who started his maritime career as a crewman on the *Sea Cloud*. His first fishing boat was the *Miss May*, followed by the *Bezo*. The *Bezo* left from a dock behind Front Street with parties of three or four charterers and sped in the direction of the Gulf Stream to troll for billfish, tuna, king mackerel and dolphin. If those fish weren't biting, Captain Sam Crayton would take his charterers to the wreck of the *Hector*, a collier that sank off Georgetown about 1900, or to the *City of Richmond*, a steel-hulled ferryboat that sank as it was being towed to the Bahamas to become a floating casino, or to some other special place to fish for channel bass, sheepshead, grouper or blackfish. Fishing was good in those days.

Yachts and Pleasure Boats

Top: A gentleman's yacht—*Sertoma* and crew. *Courtesy of Georgetown County Digital Library.*

Middle: Several yachts are tied up along Front Street, near the clock tower, in the 1920s. After World War II, the decommissioned U.S. Navy ship *Amphitrite* was moored along Front Street and used as a floating hotel. The *Amphitrite* was built in 1874 and served in the Spanish-American War and World War I. *Courtesy of Georgetown County Digital Library.*

Bottom: The Tarbox yacht *Ora Belle*, with the Georgetown waterfront in the background. *Courtesy of Georgetown County Digital Library, Tarbox Collection.*

Above: The *W.D. Morgan*, pilot schooner. *Courtesy of Georgetown County Digital Library.*

Below: Edwin Kaminski on his *Ulana II* yacht after a successful duck shoot. *Courtesy of Prevost-Kaminski Collection.*

Yachts and Pleasure Boats

Above: Gurdon Tarbox's *Ora Belle* yacht bags 57 ducks. Before limits were enforced, as many as 150 ducks might be brought down by a hunter in one day. *Courtesy of Georgetown County Digital Library, Tarbox Collection.*

Below: The hurricane of 1916 damaged many boats. The *Ora Belle* and the *Wave* were washed ashore near McClellanville. It took their crews three days to skid them back into the water. *Courtesy of Georgetown County Digital Library, Tarbox Collection.*

Above: Yacht *Ulana II* tied up along Front Street. Edwin Kaminski also owned the yachts *San Toy* and *Palmetto*. *Courtesy of Prevost-Kaminski Collection.*

Below: Big fish landed from the anchored yacht *Palmetto*. Note the unusual stern. In July 1916, Edwin Kaminski crossed Winyah Bay in *Palmetto* to warn residents of Pawleys Island of an approaching hurricane. Returning to Georgetown during the storm, the *Palmetto* sank near the pier. She was raised a few days later. *Courtesy of Prevost-Kaminski Collection.*

Yachts and Pleasure Boats

Above: Yacht *Ulana II* on Brightman's marine railway. The building in the background is the Red Store warehouse, built in 1765. *Courtesy of Prevost-Kaminski Collection.*

Below: Ladies' day aboard the steam yacht *Palmetto*. *Courtesy of Prevost-Kaminski Collection.*

Captain Sam and Rene Cathou were good friends and sometimes met at the fish house to swap stories. In 1980, the *Georgetown Times* printed a story that Captain Sam told to Rene:

> *I remember back in the early days. I once took four couples out channel bass fishing. The man who chartered the boat had quite a bit to drink. The fish weren't biting, so every few minutes he'd get up and go take a swig. After awhile, he got up again and said, "I think I'll go have a talk with the bass," and proceeded to walk off the boat. Lucky we weren't going fast or he would have drowned for sure.*
>
> *We managed to pull him in and he was still feeling no pain. Well, his wife got so mad at him for doing such a stupid thing, she picked up a big old heavy gaff and knocked him over the head. He hit the deck, out cold, you know. Then she got hysterical 'cause she thought she'd killed him. She was crying, "Oh, John, John, what have I done to you, dear?" Well, at that point I told them to pull up anchor and we headed for home.*
>
> *I didn't hear any more from the loving couple for a number of years. Then, I got a telephone call from a man wanting to charter my boat for fishing. "Remember me?" asked the gentleman. "I was the one who walked off your boat about eight years ago." I said, "I'm sorry, sir, but I just see that I'm full up for the season."*

The sport fishing boat *Bezo* trolling for game fish. *Courtesy of Ronnie Campbell.*

Relaxation aboard the yacht *Palmetto. Courtesy of Prevost-Kaminski Collection.*

Captain Sam operated the *Bezo* for many years. When he died, his fishing tackle was buried with him. Other boats soon joined the *Bezo* in the charter boat trade.

Weekend recreational fishermen have fished at North Inlet for many years. North Inlet is a small, shallow and unmarked entrance from the ocean to the north end of North Island. It joins Winyah Bay through a series of narrow, shallow creeks. North Inlet has a wild and pristine beach with no houses for miles toward the south. It can only be reached by boat, either across shallow Muddy Bay or from the ocean. Local fishermen love to go there for its beauty and isolation and to escape from civilization. North Inlet is currently part of the North Inlet–Winyah Bay Estuarine Research Reserve.

When the Intracoastal Waterway was completed, joining Maine to Florida, Georgetown became a popular stop for private yachts when traveling south to Florida and the Caribbean in the fall and back north in the spring. One yacht might decide to tie up at the Gulf or the Esso Dock, eat breakfast at Thomas' Café and shop for groceries at Ford's Store. Another yacht might tie up behind the Prince George Hotel, walk down Front Street to Kelly Khoury's Liquor Store for a bottle of bourbon, send a crewman in a taxi to the icehouse for a fifty-pound block of ice and put a dime in the slot of a payphone to order take-out from Sunset Lodge. Almost all of these yachts were wooden until the 1960s. Even in 2011, there is always the chance that an old Trumpy motor yacht or a restored Sparkman and Stevens sailing yacht might anchor or tie up in Georgetown for the night.

Georgetown was homeport for many small classic wooden pleasure boats, both power and sail. Up until the 1980s, Panther Johnson's Boatyard was located a few miles up the Sampit River, on Pennyroyal Creek. Panther had a marine railway, a few hundred feet of wharf and a big boathouse where old wooden Chris-Craft, Trojan and Elco cabin cruisers were tied up and seldom moved. Their owners occasionally dropped by on weekends to putter around their boats, drink beer and tell lies to one another. Panther had cruised into Georgetown on somebody's boat in the 1930s and never left. He leased the land on Pennyroyal Creek and built the boatyard and a house, where he lived by himself. When Cap Johnson died, the boatyard was abandoned.

Unlike Charleston, yacht and sailboat racing was never popular on Winyah Bay because of shallow depths and tidal currents. However, the Indigo Cup sailboat race, from Charleston to Georgetown, was held most years, starting in the 1960s. The starting gun for the Indigo Cup was fired from the veranda of Charleston's prestigious Carolina Yacht Club at 6:00 p.m. The boats raced past Fort Sumter, between the ship channel entrance jetties and into the ocean. The seventy-five-mile race took all night, depending on the weather. Once boats were north of lights from beach houses on Sullivan's Island and Isle of Palms, there was total darkness, except for the flashes of the powerful Charleston Light, visible for over twenty miles. Beyond that, there were no navigation lights until Georgetown Light. The Indigo Cup Race finished near the entrance to Winyah Bay, opposite Georgetown Light.

Each year, there are fewer and fewer wooden boats in Georgetown. Replicas or complete restorations of square-riggers and schooners sometimes appear for special events or pass through as training ships for navies or for schoolchildren. Some of the few remaining old wooden ships have been retired to maritime museums or became floating restaurants, but it requires much money and constant attention to keep them from rotting away, being devoured by shipworms or just sinking at their moorings, especially in southern waters, where sun and warm water speed their deterioration. A once handsome double-ended sailboat, the *Fugacity*, has been sitting on a cradle at the side of the road next to Hazard's Marina for many years. According to Jimmy Hazard, the owner of the boat just left and never came back. Inside Jimmy Hazard's house is a beautiful coffee table made from a

Yachts and Pleasure Boats

Above: Sailing ketch *Matriarch*, tied up at Cathou's railway, 1976. *Matriarch* was the author's thirty-eight-foot wooden double-ended ketch, designed by William Atkin and built in Galveston, Texas, in 1946. *Courtesy of Jerry Caines*.

Below: The author's cutter, *Exodus*, sails on Winyah Bay in 2010. *Exodus* is a 1962 gaff-rigged, thirty-foot wooden double ender, designed by William Garden and built in Tacoma, Washington. *Photo by Mary McAlister*.

barn door rudder with bronze gudgeons from some sailboat that rotted away in his boatyard.

The keel of the wooden two-masted, 140-foot pilot schooner *Spirit of South Carolina* was laid in 2001 in Charleston, but she wasn't launched until 2007, illustrating the difficulties of financing and constructing a large wooden vessel in modern times. The *Spirit of South Carolina* is a tourist attraction and school ship and has visited Georgetown several times.

Not all big boats were built directly on the waterfront. In the 1960s, E.E. Meyer built a forty-nine-foot juniper combination pleasure boat and shrimp trawler, *Spare Time*, in his Prince Street side yard, several blocks away from the water. As the boat took shape, and grew and grew, his neighbors began to accuse him of trying to duplicate Noah's Ark. When it came time to launch her, in 1966, he hooked the bow of *Spare Time* to his truck and slowly slid her down the street on logs that rolled under the keel. His friends kept moving the logs forward, but they weren't the same diameter at both ends, and the boat kept edging its way off the pavement. They finally made it to the boat ramp and into the Sampit River.

No wooden vessel larger than a runabout has been built near Georgetown for many years. Ship chandleries, like Kaminski Hardware, C.L. Ford Ship Stores and Buster Bellune's, that used to provision and sell hardware and gear to wooden ships and boats have disappeared. The old docks, boathouses and marine railways that were once scattered along the riverbanks—such as Brightman's Railway, Panther Johnson's, Jimmy Hazard's and Bucksport Marina—are gone, with the exception of the marine railway at Cathou's Fish House. Some boatyards have been converted into upscale marinas for modern yachts. The few local craftsmen who care about wooden boats and have the skill to work on them concentrate on building beautiful strip planked wooden canoes, flat-bottomed fishing skiffs or models of wooden sailing ships, or else they repair the few larger wooden boats that visit or still call Georgetown their homeport.

Nevertheless, Georgetown still has a core of wooden boat enthusiasts. Each year, the Georgetown Maritime Museum sponsors the Georgetown Wooden Boat Show. The October show has become very popular throughout the Southeast. Many boat builders and sailors participate as exhibitors. There is an annual competition by two-person teams to build identical plywood rowing skiffs as quickly and skillfully as possible and to race the completed boats across the Sampit River and back. The competition has attracted competitors from as far away as New Zealand and Canada. There are other events, including the judging of various types of wooden boats for beauty and classic design.

Boat-building contest at the 2010 Georgetown Wooden Boat Show. *Courtesy of Sally Swineford.*

The age of wooden boats is about gone. For some people, however, it is impossible to walk through a forest and not see boats in the trees. There is nothing more beautiful or more natural than a boat made of trees.

Winyah Bay remains a unique and beautiful area. Most of its shores are protected forever from further development. From the north end of North Island, southward for over sixty miles, all barrier islands are protected. The Hobcaw property on Waccamaw Neck was owned by Belle Baruch, who set up the Belle W. Baruch Foundation for the benefit of South Carolina colleges and universities to conduct research in marine biology, forestry and wildlife. Thomas Yawkey's North and South Island properties were donated to the State of South Carolina. The beaches and salt marshes along the shores of these parts of Winyah Bay will remain as they were five hundred years ago for future generations to enjoy.

HISTORY OF A WINYAH BAY PLANTATION

Fraser's Point is located on the east side of Winyah Bay, at its narrowest point. It was here that the Spanish explorer Lucas Vasquez de Ayllon is supposed to have landed in 1526. His expedition arrived in five caravels, three-masted vessels of light draft, driven by three sails, the forward two square rigged. Caravels had a high square forecastle to break the force of oncoming seas and a still higher tapering poop of two decks to provide maximum storage and living space. Three of the caravels were named *Bretorn*, *Santa Cathalina* and *Chorruca*. The five vessels carried approximately six hundred persons, including many Negro slaves. There were also eighty-nine horses, which had been disembarked, along with their riders, on the south side of the Cape Fear River. The soldiers rode their horses down the coast and joined the others at their new settlement at Fraser's Point, which they called San Miguel. The expedition had lost one ship at the entrance to the Cape Fear River, so they constructed a replacement caravel along the shore of Winyah Bay. The expedition also constructed houses for their people because Ayllon intended to use San Miguel as a base for further exploration of the coastline.

Across Winyah Bay from San Miguel was a high finger of land, a bluff bordered by freshwater swamps that drained into the bay. Winyah Indians had lived on this finger of land for probably hundreds of years, where they planted crops of maize, fished with nets, gathered oysters and hunted turkeys

Decorated Winyah Indian pottery shards found by the author along the shore of Winyah Bay, at Belle Isle. *Photo by the author.*

and deer with bows and arrows. They lived in small huts made from pine poles and thatch. They made canoes from cypress logs, using only fire and stone tools to shape the hulls. They wove cloth for mantles and blankets from the inner bark of certain trees and grasses. In winter, they wore deerskins and the furs of other animals. They made cooking and storage pots from fired clay. They had no written language. They also had no domestic animals and had never seen a horse until the Spaniards arrived.

The Winyahs helped the Spanish explorers from the time they arrived. They had never seen the sail of a ship or a white person or a metal sword. The Indians treated the Spaniards almost as gods, but the Spaniards did not respond in kind. The Catholic friars on board each ship demanded that the natives "be brought to understand the truths of our Catholic Faith." During the hot, humid summer, many of the Spaniards and Negro slaves became sick and died. Ayllon himself became sick, probably with malaria, and died on October 18, 1526. A new leader was chosen, and there was controversy among the Spaniards. This led to strife between the Spaniards and the natives, in which a number of settlers were killed. As winter approached, the Spaniards decided to abandon the settlement and return to Hispaniola. Records in Spain indicate that one of the expedition's ships, the *Capitana*, sank in Winyah Bay and that the ship carried four thousand gallons of olive oil, "stored in medium sized globular vessels with opposing handles and flaring collared mouths." Archaeologists are currently looking for the storage vessels from the *Capitana*.

The Indians across the bay had not profited from Ayllon's expedition, although they had been able to trade with them to obtain some metal for tools. Many Indians had become infected with diseases brought by the Spaniards, probably including smallpox. After Ayllon's expedition departed, the Winyahs continued to live in their settlement for another 150 years, with only an occasional interruption by Spanish or French explorers and traders. According to Spanish records, in 1605 a Spanish patrol vessel was told of a French ship entering Winyah Bay. The Spanish captain Ecija sailed to the mouth of Winyah Bay, but he reported that it was too shallow to enter.

The English arrived in Charles Towne in 1670. One of its early citizens, Thomas Smith II, had been born in England in 1664 and immigrated to Charles Towne in 1684. He made his fortune by trading with the Indians of South Carolina. It is probable that he traded arms, ammunition, liquor and other merchandise to favored Indians in return for deerskins. He also encouraged his favorite well-armed tribes to wage war against less well-armed tribes, collect prisoners and deliver them to Smith. The imprisoned Indians and the deerskins were placed aboard ships, which sailed to Barbados. The Indians were traded as slaves to sugar plantation owners in return for rum. The same ships sailed to England, where the deerskins and rum were sold. The ships then sailed to West Africa, where they took on board Negro slaves, who were delivered to Charles Towne and sold. By 1710, Smith had made enough money to buy a barony, defined as twelve thousand or more acres of land. In 1711, a land grant of twenty-four thousand acres along the western shore of Winyah Bay was made to Robert Daniell, who immediately sold it to Thomas Smith II. As owner of Winyah Barony, Smith became Thomas Landgrave Smith II.

By 1720, English and French Huguenot settlers were living along the banks of the rivers that fed into Winyah Bay. Smith foresaw an opportunity to develop his land as a town and for it to become the official port for Winyah Bay. Georgetown had not yet come into existence. Smith selected the high finger of land on the west side of Winyah Bay, where the Winyah Indians had once had their settlement, as the site for Smiths Town. The Winyah Indians were no longer there, having been enslaved, killed or driven away during Smith's trading days. In 1730, Smith raced to have his town approved by English Governor Johnson as the official port for Winyah Bay, but he was too late. Johnson had already committed to another landowner, Elisha

Screven, and he approved the present site of Georgetown as the official port for Winyah Bay.

In October 1732, Smith advertised in the *South Carolina Gazette* that he had for sale "14,000 acres of Land on Winyaw River fronting the same, most of it not above 6 miles from the Town on Sampit River." The land did not sell. Even after the present town of Georgetown was laid out in 1734, Smith continued with his plans for a competitive town. In July 1737, he placed the following advertisement, also in the *Gazette*:

> *Whereas at the request of several of the Inhabitants of the Province as well as Strangers I Landgrave Thomas Smith have laid out a Township on a Bluff of Winyah Barony containing 690 half acre Lotts fronting Winyah-River, it being about 6 Miles from Georgetown, nearer the River's Mouth. A River before the Town is about a Mile and a half wide, and generally fresh Water, whereon 500 Sail of Vessels may ride before the said Town, it being about a Mile front on the River, and contains on the Bay front 30 Lotts.*

Smiths Town did not sell. Smith died in 1738, leaving Smiths Town and other property to a son. In 1756, the acreage containing the bluff along the western shore of Winyah Bay was sold to Elias Horry, a wealthy Huguenot planter from Charles Town. Elias Horry established a rice plantation on and adjacent to the bluff and named the plantation Dover.

Elias Horry built a house on the bluff overlooking Winyah Bay and cabins for his slaves. Slaves dug the ditches, canals and water supply pond for the rice fields. Winyah Bay water at Dover was too brackish to use for irrigating rice, so the swamps on either side of the bluff were diked to impound fresh water. A deep ditch, serving as a rice canal, was dug across the high land to allow fresh water to flow from the water supply pond into the rice fields. Another canal was dug from Winyah Bay to the edge of the rice fields so that barges could transport harvested rice into Georgetown to be loaded aboard schooners and sailed to Charles Town for processing.

Elias Horry established a ferry from his Dover Plantation wharf to Calais Plantation on the other side of Winyah Bay, at Fraser's Point. The ferry route must have been named to imitate the narrow crossing of the English Channel from Dover, England, to Calais, France. The ferry enabled travelers from the south end of Waccamaw Neck to cross Winyah Bay at its narrowest point and continue toward Charles Town. He built a road from his plantation to the King's Highway, which was only a rough path between

An 1801 map of Belle Isle Plantation. North is to the left. The vertical stripes are rice fields. The lines around each rice field are dikes. The crosshatches are crop gardens. The ten small squares are slave cabins. The north–south rice irrigation canal passes between slave cabins. The circled square is labeled "dwelling." The dock and "summer house" extend into Winyah Bay. The dotted road extends west, to Kings Highway. A branch of dotted road crosses the dike, separating the water storage pond from a rice field.

Georgetown and Charles Town. He planted live oak trees along each side of the road within his plantation.

Ownership of Dover Plantation had passed into the hands of the nephew of Elias Horry II, Peter Horry, by the time of the American Revolution. Peter Horry, born in 1747, lived in Georgetown. An overseer lived in the house that Elias Horry had built, and he managed the rice plantation while Horry served under General Francis Marion during the Revolutionary War. General Peter Horry returned to Georgetown at the end of the war and wrote a memoir about his war experiences and about the life of Francis Marion. In 1801, Horry subdivided Dover Plantation into three parts, naming the 640-acre part of Dover that contained the bluff overlooking Winyah Bay and the house that Elias Horry had built Belle Isle Plantation. In 1793, Horry married Margaret Guignard, who lived most of her life, even after she was married, in Columbia, South Carolina.

Horry also owned a house on North Island, where he lived each summer. Peter Horry was a large man of over three hundred pounds. He traveled back and forth between Georgetown and North Island and his rice plantations by boat, rowed or sailed by his slaves. During the year 1812, Horry kept a journal describing his life on North Island. Starting with the entry on June 17, 1812:

Rose very Early, & all my Servants & Getting Ready for Embarkation & Sent my Bedd Chain, bed Benches, boards…Breakfasted Early & all hands went on board about 8 Oclock—a Promising Passage (a fine day) Stoped at Dover to take in 2 Oarsmen—made our Passage from Dover to So Inlet in 3 hours found my Carpenters forward Repairing my House…I found my Room very Cold Did Not Sleep well—

Tuesday 15th July 1812—Just before Sun Set I Got into My Sedan & was Carried to the Sea beach & around to the Bason…

Thursday, Rose in Tolerable spirits, arranged my Negroes to flat & boat Going up, the first to Dover, the other to George Town to my House…Issac has directions to repair Immediately my Small boat at Dover to be brought here to Catch fish, Clamps—Oysters, Crabs &c…Miss Maria Visited me Last Night for an hour. She was Inviting, & I felt myself. But alas; the Thought of Sinning (Altho' the Devil Tempted me) prevailed & my better Sense Predominated—

Thursday, July 25, Boat men went Early to fish, having Clams, therefore only Shrimps wanting…Boat carried up Conks & Sea Mud & went off about 9 Oclock. 3 Oarsmen. & 2 Sails—& was soon out of Sight, Tide Favorable…

July 27, Wind very high at No. East for Sometime past & now tis heavy, Drisling Cloudy weather—I Look for a heavy Gale from the No East, or East Quarter & directly from Sea—so Marriners on our Coasts. Be Vigilent on board your Vessells Keep all lights & Sails Close reefed & Bowlings all Clear, boats Secured on Deck & Experienced men, at your helm & Good Night Watch, & Lights in Benecles—to See your Compass & then I & you will Expect to Weather all—Sailors is Like Souldiers—Sometimes Lead Lazy Lives & Sometimes, hard times Overtakes them & dangers & difficulties Succeeds—but hearts of Oak my brave Lads. Stand to it & trust to him that made you, we must all Die—but be Comforted for we Cant die before our times are Come 'tis Decreed & then we Go. To a Land of Rest. Free from all Cares & Trouble for Evermore amen—This afternoon about 2 Oclock discovered a 3 Mast Vessell Standin for the Light House could discover that her Colors was hoisted but could not discover of what Nation about 4 Oclock PM. She stood off to the Eastward & Soon was out of Sight, I Suppose her of force & Cruising on our Coast to Meet an Enemies Vessell—I hope She is an American—

Thursday, July 30, 1812, Rode out & Got some wood & returned home found Mr. Mitchell at my house. He Stayed & breakfasted with me, *however before he did so; he Asked for a Julop; my Servant Rachal handed him, Brandy Sugar & water. I Soon found it 'fected his head, he Eat very Little at breakfast; a Decanter of Brandy, he Ordered to be placed on a Small Table Near to the One on which we were breakfasting on—he had frequently recourse to this decanter & Soon he realed to & fro—Laid down in a Room on a bed frequently, I found his Language, was Extremely defective, he Stammered, & his Eyes half Closed—At this Instant he is Asleep on a Bed in a Spare Room—I Gave Rachael directions not to Wake him, As he Spoke of Swimming in the Sea—a shark would Soon Cutt him to pieces—I Sincerely Pity this Otherwise Most Valuable Gentleman Planter & Attorney at Law—but Alass, he is Lost to himself, his friends & Country Liquor, Oh Liquor what Mischief has thou Occasioned in the World.—*

Friday, August 14, Viewed the painting of my big boat, which is to my Liking; if no Rain today, the boat will be finished & be handsomely Painted, when I may form Parties of Ladies on fishing Matches & if they Carry beaus, may have also Courting Matches; the Latter will be most Agreeable to the bells—if beau's do not make Advances, Bells rather there Continue Scratching & biting, do you make Such, for when you are Married what Signifies which made the first Proposals—the Knot being once Tyed who can undo it—Then fall to work night and day, until the Kegg is Filled, thus will you my Good Girls answer the End of your Creation—

Sunday, August 23, 1812:...I am of Opinion our Ships of War ought to Act only in the American Coasts in Protection of our Trade & Guard our own Ships & harbors—The English are too Powerful for us in the Uropean Seas—On our own Coasts we have many Advantages over them.—& their Wt. Indies Trade is well worth the attention of our Armed Vessells—the Produce of their Islands to us are of Great Value—& their Vessells are in our Power very often to Capture & Soon are Safe in our harbours. This is the Game we ought to play with the British, our Ships are well built for Sailing & our Seamen are Equal to any in the world—In this way our brave Lads Let's have at them.—

Tuesday, August 25: I Saw this morning at Sea but near the beach two amazing Fish—Large & almost Round, Swimmed near the Surface of the water—I knew it not, Perhaps It may be a Devil fish, such I have heard Off—Many Persons both Whites & black Came to behold Such Monstrous Large fishes—& we all Stared at such Uncommon fishes—

Horry returned to his house in Brown Town (part of Georgetown) in October 1812. On Wednesday, November 4, 1812:

I with the Miss Bays & Cheesborough Visited Belle Isle Plantation & we dined there, I saw my pounding Mill, 'tis near finished I saw our Garden & Barn yard & Potatoe Houses—I Saw my Driver & I delivered out 28 pairs shoes to my Negroes—I fear my Crop will be a very Small One—I hear'd that my Rice Sent by Capt Marsh has Arrived Safe at Charleston— We returned home about Sun Set—

Peter Horry built a new house in Columbia, South Carolina, in 1813, sold his houses in Georgetown and on North Island and moved to Columbia. When Peter Horry died in Columbia in 1815 at the age of sixty-nine, he willed the Belle Isle Plantation property to his wife, Margaret Guignard Horry. Peter and Margaret had no children. When Margaret died in 1817, a niece, Sarah Bay, inherited Belle Isle. Sarah Bay married William Mayrant, a cotton planter whose plantation was near Columbia. The Belle Isle rice plantation continued to be managed by an overseer who lived on the property. The highest part of the bluff, overlooking Winyah Bay, became known as Mayrants Bluff. The Mayrants' eldest daughter, Sarah, married William Richardson in 1844, and they were given Belle Isle Plantation. When the Civil War started in 1861, Belle Isle was still producing large quantities of rice and still had a slave population of more than fifty.

At the beginning of the war, batteries of cannons were constructed on South Island and Cat Island to protect Winyah Bay. However, they were too remote and too far apart to be effective, and there were not enough forces to man the batteries, so they were abandoned. When Union gunboats began to enter Winyah Bay in 1862, the Confederate commanding generals decided to construct new batteries on both sides of the narrowest part of the bay, at Mayrants Bluff on Belle Isle Plantation and at Fraser's Point, on the other side of the bay. Construction of the battery on Mayrants Bluff started in August 1862. Slave labor moved several thousand cubic yards of earth to construct gun emplacements for ten cannons and the necessary ammunition storage bunkers, ditches, barracks and stables. The completed battery, named Battery White, was a formidable fortress. Another smaller series of gun emplacements was constructed at the rear of Belle Isle Plantation to guard against land attack.

The Confederacy had a shortage of both cannons and soldiers to man them. When Battery White was completed in November 1862, General

Beauregard had just been placed in charge of the coastal defenses of the Carolinas. He immediately began to receive requests for more men to man Battery White and other Winyah Bay defenses. As the war wore on, these requests became more and more urgent. One detachment of cavalry and one of artillery were manning the nine-gun fortification at Battery White, but desertions were high and enlistments were short and not renewed. During 1863, blockade-running ships were using Murrells Inlet, north of Georgetown, as a port to land supplies and take away cotton and salt. Union ships made several sorties into Murrells Inlet to destroy blockade runners, and troops had to be pulled away from Battery White to defend Murrells Inlet.

In May 1863, Battery White was placed under the command of Captain Franz Melchers, who brought with him an artillery company of German immigrants from Charleston. From the beginning, Melchers had severe problems because of the desertion of his men, who would have much preferred to remain in Charleston. In addition, sickness, boredom and bickering among the men, including the officers in charge, contributed to the problems of Battery White. No Union ships ever attacked, and there was never a reason for Battery White to fire its cannons in anger. In fact, the Union navy didn't need to pass in front of Battery White. In April 1864, the steamship USS *Cimarron* anchored in Winyah Bay and landed thirty sailors, who hiked through the woods into Georgetown and set fire to a rice mill and five thousand bushels of rice. Even so, General Trapier, in overall charge of the Georgetown area, pleaded with General Beauregard and Governor Bonham for more troops and larger guns for Battery White. Two ten-inch Columbiad cannons were sent, but after Gettysburg, more troops were taken away from Battery White to fight in Virginia.

In early 1864, Captain Melchers reported severe shortages of ammunition and equipment. Desertions and disputes at Battery White continued. Six German soldiers in Melcher's company rowed out to a Union blockading ship, defected and declared allegiance to the Union. In March 1864, thirty-five-year-old Lieutenant James Wortham, who had been elected state senator in 1862, challenged Lieutenant Mayham Ward, brother of the company commander, to a duel. The duel didn't take place, and Wortham was court-martialed.

The company commander of the Waccamaw Light Artillery, Captain Joshua Ward, and his brother, Lieutenant Mayham Ward, both stationed at Battery White in 1864, were prime examples of the downfall of the rice planter empire. They had inherited from their father, Joshua John Ward, who died in 1853, the two richest and largest rice plantations in the area (what is now Brookgreen Gardens and Hobcaw Barony) and the most slaves (over 1,000), and yet they were serving undistinguished careers in the remote military post of Battery White. Both would lose everything they had after the war. In July 1864, Captain Joshua Ward resigned his commission, citing health reasons, and moved to England. Lieutenant Mayham Ward then took over as commander and immediately requested furlough, saying 20 of his slaves had run away to join the Union navy and he wanted to check on his remaining 360 servants. He suggested that another brother, twenty-three-year-old Sergeant Benjamin Ward, could take over the company. In September 1864, the fewer than 50 remaining men of the Waccamaw Light Artillery were transferred to guard several thousand Union prisoners, who were being moved from the Andersonville, Georgia prison to a new location, leaving the few remaining men of Captain Melcher's company. They were ordered to defend Battery White "to the last extremity," but they were also told to spike the guns and bring the men to Mount Pleasant if necessary to save their lives.

In February 1865, some deserters from Battery White told the commander of the USS *Mingoe* that Battery White had been abandoned. The *Mingoe*, a side-wheel vessel mounting eleven cannons, steamed up Winyah Bay and fired four rounds into Battery White. Receiving no response, the *Mingoe* anchored and sent a landing party of marines ashore. Battery White was abandoned, except for fifteen deserters from the German artillery, who immediately surrendered to the troops of the *Mingoe*. Captain Melchers had obeyed orders, and all sixteen of the cannons had been spiked, but a large amount of artillery ammunition and equipment had been left. The Union marines carried off what they could use, dismounted the guns, broke the carriages and scattered everything else.

In late February, Admiral Dahlgren visited Battery White and commented that the fortification was "well planned and carefully executed" and "if the Works had been sufficiently manned, it would have required good troops to take the work." He also commented, "The grounds occupied by these works might be one hundred acres, beautifully wooded with live oak," and that "huts for the men were numerous and well constructed with ranges of stalls for horses." On March 1, Admiral Dahlgren's flagship, *Harvest Moon*, struck a mine in Winyah Bay and sank.

During the entire war, the overseer of Belle Isle Plantation continued to live in the existing plantation house and to plant rice with the slaves who hadn't escaped and turned themselves over to Union troops. At the end of the war, all slaves were freed and the production of rice at Belle Isle ceased. When Union marines left Battery White, it fell into ruin and was never again used as a fortification.

History of a Winyah Bay Plantation

When Nathaniel Bishop paddled his canoe past Belle Isle Plantation, in 1875:

> [He] *followed the shores of Winyah Bay toward the sea. Near Battery White, on the right shore, in the pine forests, was the birthplace of Marion, the brave patriot of the American revolution, whose bugle call summoned the youth of those days to arms.*
>
> *When near the inlet, the rice-plantation marshes skirted the shore for some distance. Out of these wet lands flowed a little stream, called Mosquito Creek, which once connected the North Santee River with Winyah Bay.*

Bishop turned into Mosquito Creek and continued toward Charleston.

In 1893, Gardner B. Penniman, a wealthy member of New York society, married Mary Johnstone, whose family had owned Estherville Plantation, south of Dover, from the mid-1700s until after the Civil War. Looking for a summer home in 1894, the Pennimans bought the abandoned rice fields, burned-out house, falling-down slave cabins and all of the trash and disorder of thirty years of neglect at Belle Isle Plantation. Their purchase, including several other adjacent plantations, totaled seven thousand acres. Mrs. Penniman, who was an avid gardener, envisioned a restored antebellum plantation with pathways of flowering camellias, azaleas and magnolias. In 1905, she began the planting of what would become the beautiful and famous Belle Isle Gardens. The Pennimans built a three-story, fourteen-room house overlooking Winyah Bay. The house had cypress shingle siding and a metal standing seam roof. Francis Johnstone Jr., Mary Johnstone Penniman's nephew, visited the house when he was a boy and described the living room:

> *The living room was my fondest memory. On the floor, in front of the fireplace, was a grizzly bear rug with a realistically mounted head attached. Over the fireplace, above a massive oak mantle was mounted a large moose head. On the opposite wall, a bald eagle with spread wings appeared to be swooping down on the bear rug. In addition, there were several other assorted animals mounted on the walls. These animal relics were Uncle Gardiner's big game hunting trophies.*

The Pennimans also owned a large home on Long Island and a fox-hunting estate in Ireland.

Gardiner Penniman sold Belle Isle and his other Winyah Bay property to B. Walker Cannon in 1917. Mr. Cannon was only interested in the part of the property that had timber that could be cut and sold for lumber, so in 1919 he sold 250 acres, which contained Belle Isle Gardens and the house, to

Frank Johnstone, cousin of Mary Penniman. Georgetonian Frank Johnstone and his family moved into the Penniman house. He continued to improve and expand the gardens, and in 1925, he opened them to the public and charged admission to see them.

A few years later, Mr. and Mrs. Henry M. Sage of Albany, New York, visited Belle Isle Gardens, and Mrs. Sage was smitten by its beauty. Mr. Sage had inherited a profitable lumber and real estate business from his father and was a very wealthy man. He had served in the New York Senate and had run for governor. He had married his second wife, Cornelia Cogswell Sage, in 1911. Soon after their visit to Belle Isle, Mr. Sage suffered a stroke and was an invalid until he died in 1933. Mrs. Sage, who was in control of vast sums of money, pursued her desire to possess Belle Isle Plantation and Gardens. In 1929, she and her husband leased Belle Isle Gardens, the house and 238 acres from Frank Johnstone for a period of ten years. As allowed by the lease, Mrs. Sage demolished the existing fourteen-room Penniman house. Mrs. Sage then purchased the Mendenhall House, a large and historic early nineteenth-century house in Newberry, South Carolina, and had it dismantled, then reassembled and added onto at Belle Isle, with a sweeping view of Winyah Bay. She planted many more flowers and shrubs, some atop the old fortifications of Battery White.

Frank Johnstone had saved many of the timbers from the demolished Penniman house, which he reused in building his family a large house just north of the gardens that he named Mount Hope. However, Johnstone lost his money during the Great Depression, and by 1939, Mount Hope was in foreclosure. Needing a place for his family to live, Frank Johnstone refused to renew the Belle Isle lease or sell the property to Mrs. Sage. In desperation, Mrs. Sage purchased Dover Plantation, directly south of Belle Isle. There was no house at Dover. In 1939, the new Santee River dam at Moncks Corner, South Carolina, was under construction. At its completion in 1940, Lakes Moultrie and Marion would be formed, flooding thousands of acres of land, including most of the old Santee Canal and several historic plantation houses. Mrs. Sage purchased the 1810 Woodlawn Plantation house before it could be flooded. Woodlawn, according to previous owner Percival Ravenel Porcher, "was the finest house between the Santee and the Cooper Rivers." Mrs. Sage had the house dismantled and the parts numbered, stored, transported to Dover and reassembled overlooking Winyah Bay.

Frank Johnstone Sr. and his family moved back into the Belle Isle house, minus the staircase and a few other parts that Mrs. Sage had taken with her to Dover. Unfortunately, the Belle Isle house burned to the ground in 1942.

Mary Shower and Ned Shower are looked after by a Johnstone maid. In the background is the house that Mrs. Henry Sage moved from Newberry and rebuilt. The photograph was taken in 1942, a few months before the house burned. *Courtesy of Mary Shower McAlister.*

Johnstone continued to maintain and show the gardens to visitors. In 1944, President Franklin Roosevelt visited Belle Isle Gardens while he was staying with Bernard Baruch at Hobcaw Barony, across Winyah Bay. When Frank Johnstone Sr. died, his son Bill Johnstone and his family built a smaller house at Belle Isle and continued to show the gardens. However, after the blooming season for azaleas and camellias was over and the heat and mosquitoes of summer arrived, there were few visitors and not nearly enough admission revenue to pay for upkeep of the gardens. Bill and his brother and sister sold off portions of the back property as house lots. Only the gardens and Battery White were left untouched.

In 1972, Bill Johnstone sold the remaining seventy-five acres, including the gardens and Battery White, to a development partnership, which proposed a retirement and second-home condominium community at Belle Isle. A Charleston architecture firm, Lucas and Stubbs, planned the layout and design of the condominium buildings and amenities in such a way as to cause minimum interference with over fifty magnificent live oak trees and paths with hundreds of azalea and camellia bushes. The buildings were situated in open spaces within the garden and along the shores of the lakes. Battery White, which was listed on the National Register of Historic Places, remained untouched.

The master plan called for a marina along the shore of Winyah Bay as the primary amenity for the community. A ten-acre, high marsh site was selected for the marina. The marsh site had been used by the U.S. Army Corps of Engineers as a spoil area when the Winyah Bay ship channel was being dredged in the 1940s. The marina site was surveyed and found to be above mean high tide, as required. An environmental impact report was prepared, and applications for dredging and marina permits were filed in 1973. The U.S. Department of the Interior issued an objection to the marina that stayed in place for a year. No development work could start until the marina permit was approved. The developers had exhausted all means of convincing the Department of the Interior to drop its objection, except political ones. The developers' environmental lawyer finally scheduled a meeting with Senator Strom Thurmond in his Washington office. As the developers kneeled on the floor of his office, spreading out their plans, Thurmond ordered one of his attractive young female interns to summon an assistant secretary of the interior. The secretary arrived and sat on a footstool in front of Strom's massive swivel chair. Strom looked down at him and said, "Can't you help out these poor South Carolina country boys?" That was all it took. Within a few weeks, the permits were issued and construction began.

The one-year delay had been costly to the developer. By the time the first phase of condominium construction at Belle Isle had been completed in 1975, an oil embargo in the Middle East had tripled the price of gasoline and effectively stopped vacation and second-home sales across America. The development was stalled for a little while, threatening to become another Smiths Town, but by 1985, all of the town house condominiums had been sold and were occupied by retirement and second-home buyers. They had been attracted to Belle Isle by the tranquil beauty of its trees, flowers, birds and lakes; by views of the marshes, Winyah Bay and the distant lighthouse; and by the mystery of the abandoned earthworks of Battery White.

Today, the sight of a full moon rising across Winyah Bay is as beautiful to the current Belle Isle owners as it was for the Winyah Indians, Thomas Smith, Elias and Peter Horry, Mary Penniman, Cornelia Sage, Frank and Bill Johnstone and maybe even a few of the Confederate soldiers at Battery White.

GLOSSARY OF NAUTICAL TERMS

BARK OR BARQUE: a sailing vessel with three or more masts, with fore and aft sails on the aftermost mast and square sails on the other masts

BATEAU: a shallow draft, flat-bottomed boat

BEAM: the width of a ship at its widest point

BEAM-END: a vessel, heeled over at ninety degrees

BINNACLE: a stand on the deck of a ship, in front of the helmsman, in which navigational instruments are placed

BOOM: the spar at the foot of a sail

BOOM JAW: the fitting that attaches the boom to the mast

BOSUN: the most skilled seaman of a ship in handling lines and working on deck

BOWSPRIT: a spar projecting from the bow of a vessel

BREECHES BUOY: a rope-based rescue device stretching from ship to shore or ship to ship

BRIGANTINE OR BRIG: a vessel with two masts, only the forward of which is square rigged

BURGEE: a distinguishing flag flown from the top of a mast of a ship

CEILING: the internal planking of a ship

CLEW: lower and outer corner of a fore-and-aft sail

CLIPPER SHIP: a fast sailing ship of the nineteenth century with three or more masts, all square rigged

COLLIER: a bulk cargo ship that carried coal

CROSSTREES: two horizontal struts at the height where the mast joins the topmast of a schooner

CUTTER: a small single-masted sailboat with two or more headsails

DONKEY ENGINE: a steam or internal combustion engine on a schooner for the purpose of raising sails, raising anchors and driving pumps

DORY: a small boat with a flat bottom

DOUBLE-ENDED BOAT: a boat that is pointed, both at the bow and the stern

DRAFT: the vertical distance between the waterline and the bottom of the keel

DRIFTPIN: a spike used to fasten heavy keel members

FLAT: a rectangular, flat-bottomed boat with square ends

FORECASTLE OR FOC'SL: living quarters for the common seaman, located in a cabin near the bow of a ship; the galley and donkey engine were also located there

FORESTAYSAIL: the triangular aftermost headsail of a schooner

FRAME: one of the curved, transverse members of a ship's structure, branching outward and upward from the keel

FREEBOARD: the height of a ship's deck above the waterline

FRIGATE: any of several types of sailing warships

GAFF: spar to which the head of a four-sided fore-and-aft sail is attached

GUDGEON: metal clamp bolted to the stern-post; pintles on the rudder fit into corresponding holes in the gudgeons

HARBOR FURL: to neatly gather in a sail and secure it with gaskets to the yard, boom, spar or mast

HAWSER: a rope or cable

JETTY: stone structure projecting outward from a harbor entrance

JIB: triangular sail set on a stay before the foremast, extending from the jib boom or bowsprit

JIB BOOM: spar extending the bowsprit and taking a forward stay and the foot of the forward jib

JOLLY BOAT: small but strongly built boat stowed aboard ship

KEEL: principal length of timber in a ship, running fore and aft; the keel supports and unites the whole structure

KEELSON: internal keel mounted over the floor timbers, above the main keel, providing additional structural strengthening

KETCH: a sailing craft with two masts, a mainmast and a shorter mizzenmast, abaft of the mainmast but forward of the rudder post

LAUNCH: a large motorboat

LIGHTER: a large flat-bottomed barge to deliver goods to a cargo ship

LIGHTSHIP: a stationary vessel acting as a lighthouse, placed offshore

MIZZENMAST: third mast from forward in a vessel with three or more masts

OAKUM: substance made from old ropes, unraveled, loosened and picked apart, used in caulking seams and planks

PERIAGUA: a small wooden boat that can be sailed or rowed; some were made by splitting a dugout canoe and extending the bottom and sides

PITCH: dark resinous substance distilled from tar; used in caulking seams

PORT: left-hand side of a ship, looking forward

PROW: the pointed stem or beak of a ship

RUNNING LIGHT: a navigation light, red on the port side, green on the starboard side; white lights are at the stern and forward of the foremost mast

SCHOONER: a sailing vessel characterized by fore and aft sails on two or more masts, with the forward mast being no taller than the rear masts

SHEER-LEG: triangular structure consisting of two upright spars lashed together at the top, the lower ends spread out, the whole steadied by guys, used for lifting loads

SHEET: rope or chain attached to the clews of sails to extend them or hold them in place

SKIFF: a small boat

SLOOP: a sailboat with a fore and aft rig and a single mast farther forward than the mast of a cutter

SPANKER: a gaff-rigged fore and aft sail, set from and aft of the aftermost mast

SPAR: general term for a rounded length of timber, such as a yard, gaff or boom

SQUARE-RIG: a generic type of sail and rigging arrangement in which the primary driving sails are carried on horizontal spars, which are perpendicular to the keel of the vessel and to the masts

STARBOARD: right-hand side of a ship, looking forward

STAY: rope that sustains a mast in a fore and aft direction

SUNSET LODGE: an internationally famous house of prostitution existing on the outskirts of Georgetown from the 1920s until 1969

TEREDOS: a type of shipworm that bores holes in wooden vessels

THROAT HALYARD: rope or tackle used to hoist the inboard end of a gaff and its part of the sail

TONNAGE: measure of the cargo-carrying capacity of a vessel

TOPMAST: mast mounted above the lower mast; second part of a complete mast

TOPSAIL SCHOONER: a traditional schooner that carries additional fore and aft triangular sails above the gaffs of the mainsails

TREENAILS: cylindrical wooden pin used to fix a ship's planks to its frames

WARDROOM: the compartment on a ship where the officers took their meals

WINCH: horizontal revolving barrel used to give mechanical advantage in working a purchase to hoist cargo or sails

YAWL BOAT: a small ship's boat, usually rowed by four or six oars

BIBLIOGRAPHY

Atkin, William. *Of Yachts and Men*. Dobbs Ferry, NY: Sheridan House, Inc., 1949.

Bishop, Nathaniel H. *Voyage of the Paper Canoe*. Boston: Lee and Shephard, 1878.

Bostick, Douglas W. *Sunken Plantations*. Charleston, SC: The History Press, 2008.

Bridwell, Ronald E. *Gem of the Atlantic Seaboard*. Georgetown, SC: Georgetown Times, 1991.

Browning, Robert M., Jr. *Success Is All That Was Expected*. Dulles, VA: Potomac Books, Inc., 2002.

Burgess, Robert H. *Cruising Schooner*. Newport News: University Press of Virginia, 1978.

————. *Sea, Sails and Shipwreck*. Cambridge, MD: Tidewater Publishers, 1970.

Coker, P.C., III. *Charleston's Maritime Heritage 1670–1865*. Charleston, SC: CokerCraft Press, 1987.

Drayton, Governor John. *A View of South Carolina*. Charleston, SC, 1802.

Estep, H. Cole. *How Wooden Ships Are Built*. Cleveland, OH: Penton Publishing Co., 1918.

Fleetwood, William C., Jr. *Tidecraft*. Tybee Island, GA: WBG Marine Press, 1995.

Garden, William. *Yacht Design*. St. Michaels, MD: Tiller Publishing, 1998.

Greenhill, Basil, and Denis Stonham. *Seafaring under Sail*. Cambridge, UK: City Press, 1981.

Greenhill, Basil, and Sam Manning. *The Schooner* Bertha L. Downs. London: Naval Institute Press, 1995.

Johnson, Harry, and Frederick S. Lightfoot. *Maritime New York*. New York: Dover Publications, 1980.

Kaiser, Fred. *Built on Honor, Sailed with Skill*. Ann Arbor, MI: Sarah Jennings Press, 1989.

Lachicotte, Alberta. *Rice Plantations*. Georgetown, SC: Georgetown County Historical Society, 1955.

Lawson, Dennis T. *Atlantic Coast Lumber Corporation*. Georgetown, SC: Rice Museum, 1975.

Leigh, Jack. *Oystering*. Charleston, SC: Carolina Art Association, 1983.

Lewis, James A. *Neptune's Militia*. Kent, OH: Kent State University Press, 1999.

McAlister, Mac, and Mary McAlister. *Cruising Through Life*. Independence, VA: Ross Editorial, 2003.

Nautical Terms under Sail. New York: Crown Publishers, Inc., 1978.

Porcher, F.A. *The Santee Canal*. Charleston: South Carolina Historical Society, 1903.

Prevost, Charlotte Kaminski. *Pawleys Island*. Columbia, SC: The State Printing Co., 1972.

Quattlebaum, Paul. *The Land Called Chicora*. Gainesville: University of Florida Press, 1956.

Rogers, George C., Jr. *The History of Georgetown County, South Carolina*. Columbia: University of South Carolina Press, 1970.

Simms, William Gilmore. *The Life of Francis Marion*. Charleston, SC: The History Press, 2007.

Slocum, Joshua. *Voyage of the* Liberdade. N.p.: Grenada Publishing, 1948.

Snow, Ralph, and Douglas Lee. *A Shipyard in Maine*. Bath, ME: Tilbury House, Publishers, 1999.

Unger, Harlow Giles. *Lafayette*. Hoboken, NJ: John Wiley & Sons, Inc., 2002.

Waterhouse, Richard. *A New World Gentry*. Charleston, SC: The History Press, 2005.

Wolff, Geoffrey. *The Hard Way Around*. New York: Alfred A. Knopf, 2010.

INDEX